REMEMBER - IT'S ALL IN THE FACE.

2007

It's More Than Words - Reading People From The Outside In

The Astonishing Power of Face Reading

by

Harry Perdew, Ph.D.

Bloomington, IN Milton Keynes, UK

AuthorHouse™
1663 Liberty Drive, Suite 200
Bloomington, IN 47403
www.authorhouse.com
Phone: 1-800-839-8640

AuthorHouse™ UK Ltd.
500 Avebury Boulevard
Central Milton Keynes, MK9 2BE
www.authorhouse.co.uk
Phone: 08001974150

First published by AuthorHouse 8/22/2006

ISBN: 1-4259-4074-9 (sc)

Library of Congress Control Number: 2006905563

Printed in the United States of America
Bloomington, Indiana

This book is printed on acid-free paper.

Please direct all correspondence and inquires to:
The Perdew Group
P.O. Box 1446
Chino Hills, CA 91709-2004
Phone: 909-606-1880; Fax 909-393-5711
Website: www.harryperdew.com Email: info@harryperdew.com

Preface

Since 1982, I have traveled the globe, learning and sharing information along the way. I have met many people from nearly every walk of life—some famous, some infamous, some innovative executives, some skilled craftsmen, some outstanding salespeople, some millionaires, some poor, some college educated and some street educated. I committed myself to learn something important from each person, regardless of his or her situation.

As a change navigator who specializes in teaching people how to understand and use nonverbal communication, I felt a special need to search out and identify the everyday principles of communicating that lead to a happy and successful life. In this way, I hope to add value and substance to the service I deliver to my clients.

Over the last fifteen years, I have sorted through and organized many of the things I have learned as a business executive, entrepreneur, teacher, husband, and father. What you hold in your hands is a reflection of that work. I sincerely hope it will be of benefit to you—that it will inspire you and increase your personal and professional happiness as you begin *to understand and use the nonverbal communication ideas presented in this book. I promise you, after reading a few pages, you will never look at a face the same way again.*

Harry Perdew, Ph.D.

Proviso

T his book is designed to provide information about nonverbal communication. It is not the purpose of this book to reprint all the information that is available on the topic. This book should complement, augment, and enhance other writings. The reader is urged to read all the available material and learn as much as possible about the art and science of face reading, and then adapt the information to their individual needs.

Every effort has been made to make this book as accurate and complete as possible. However, there may be typos and mistakes in content. For that reason, this book should only be used as a general guide and not as the definitive source for face reading information.

The purpose of this book is to educate and entertain. The author assumes no liability or responsibility to any person or entity with respect to any loss or damage caused or alleged to be caused, directly or indirectly, by the information and illustrations in this book.

Contents

Acknowledgements

I would like to thank all the people who shared their faces with me. Their valuable feedback, shared insights, and personal openness helped validate the information contained in this book. Their generous input is reflected throughout this book.

I want to share a particular thanks to my wife, Charlene, who was always there to shore up anything that began to unravel. Her patience with my unending prattle about each face I saw wherever we traveled was enormous. She was always there with a kind word or a kick in the rear whenever it was needed. Without her cajoling and encouragement, this book would not have been written.

Special thanks to Judy Marsh for her encouragement and suggestions, and Rebecca Ewing for her very sage and professional input. Their valuable contributions helped make this endeavor a better piece of work.

Finally I want to thank all those current day pioneers and masters of physiognomy: Mac Fulfer, J.D., Rose Rosetree, and Naomi Tickle, from whose work much of the material in this book is based.

Introduction

"A man's face as a rule says more, and more interesting things, than his mouth, for it is a compendium of everything his mouth will ever say, in that it is the monogram of all this man's thoughts and aspirations." ~ Arthur Schopenhauer

In the many years I've spent working with people as a business executive, entrepreneur, teacher, husband, and father, I've found that there is one thread that permeates everything I have experienced. That thread is communication, or rather the inability to communicate well. We, as a species, simply do not have the ability to tell someone in words exactly what we are really trying to communicate. We just haven't evolved enough yet. So we must rely on the forms of communication we used before we had language to help us better understand one another.

Our intuition about people's temperaments, feelings, and intentions depend on what we observe in their faces and body language. We are all intuitive people readers from birth.

We are all hardwired from birth to communicate without words. Before we had language, we communicated by observing the face and body movement of the other person. "Do I recognize them?" "What are their intentions?" "Are they friendly or are they going to harm me?"

Recent studies of infants have shown that they have the ability to recognize their mothers when shown a series of pictures that included their mother and other women. A portion of the baby's brain actually lights up when it sees a picture of its mother's face. In fact, doesn't a baby communicate with its parents without words for many months until it begins to learn how to use words?

Researchers have found that 93 percent of communication is nonverbal. That means the words we use are only 7 percent of what we are trying to say. To become effective communicators, we have to learn and master the skills of nonverbal communication.

Understanding the nonverbal is a means to better communication with every person we meet. Whether managing, selling, hiring, negotiating, speaking, or interacting, the ability to determine another's attitude and frame of mind is a skill from which everyone can benefit.

Mastering the skills of nonverbal communication is a valuable tool for business owners, managers, salespeople, attorneys, human resource professionals, politicians, mediators, counselors, consultants, parents, teachers, physicians, psychiatrists, therapists, criminologists, receptionists, nurses, public relations professionals, writers, public speakers, and anyone who wants to persuade with conviction.

"A convincing illustration of the power of nonverbal communication is the unparalleled political popularity experienced by Ronald Reagan, who very early in his presidency was dubbed the 'Great Communicator." ~ (Burgoon et al. 1989:4).

Physiognomy, the scientific name for face reading, is the art and science of one of the most important communication skills we can learn. Face reading is an extremely accurate way to effectively identify and analyze the features of the face that characterize personality traits in people.

Chapter 1
FACE READING

*"To acquire knowledge, one must study;
but to acquire wisdom, one must observe."*
~ Marilyn vos Savant

Face reading has been fascinating people as long as people have been trying to communicate. It is possible to read the unrevealed story of people's lives and their personalities by using the ancient and modern knowledge of face reading.

The style of physiognomy used in this book is a combination of Western, Chinese, and Indian knowledge. This face reading information has been collected and studied for thousands of years to gain insight into the connection between a person's facial features and personality.

The most distinctive, most recognizable, and most memorable feature of any human being is the face. We all understand the importance of facial expression in communication. We know the meaning of a smile or a frown, but the face is also a living record and personality profile of each individual. In its features and lines, each face reflects its owner's personal history, mental attitudes, character traits, intimacy requirements, work ethic, personal preferences, and much more.

Like every personality, each face is distinctive and unique. The idea that the features of the face and its owner's personality must in some way be related has captivated people since the search for knowledge began, and it is still as compelling today.

Consciously or not, we all make judgments about other people's faces. We say that someone has an honest face or puts on a brave face. When we first see or meet someone, we immediately make what we think are accurate judgments about that person, but because we often reach those assumptions instinctively and without much thought, we are usually wrong.

The study of reading character from facial features—the science of physiognomy—began in China, where it is known as xiang mian, (saing mien) and kan xiang. In India physiognomy is referred to as Mukha Lakshana Shastra. Even in the West, detailed attention to the science of interpreting people's character from their faces dates back to the time of the classical scholars Aristotle, Plato, Aristophanes, Hippocrates, and Pliny, who all wrote at length about the subject. In Imperial Rome, face reading was considered a very honorable profession.

Scholars from Europe also subscribed to the science. These observations are mentioned in the Jewish *Cabala*, Chaucer, Shakespeare, Bacon, Milton, and Dryden. Many of their philosophical followers made popular use of physiognomic theory and principles. It continued to attract some of the world's greatest minds, including detailed research into face reading by the father of the theory of evolution, Charles Darwin.

Toward the end of the eighteenth century, Johann Kaspar Lavater, a pastor and poet in Zurich, undertook the task of classifying facial features along with mental abilities and inclinations. His essays and superb illustrations in physiognomy became a major resource in the field, and he became known as the discoverer of this "new" science.

In the 1930s, Los Angeles US Superior Court Judge Dr. Edward Vincent Jones observed the behavioral patterns of people who appeared before him in court. He became so intrigued by his observations that he left his judicial work and began to research the field using works that were published by Lavater and other notable authors on the subject.

Using established scientific principles, Jones looked at 200 different facial features and later narrowed the number down to 68. His studies also included the hands and body proportions. During the 1960s, a colleague of Jones's, newspaper editor Robert Whiteside, conducted research on 1,028 study participants to determine the accuracy for personality profiling. He and his colleagues found physiognomy to be 92 percent accurate for personality profiling.

Today physiognomy has become a legitimate field of re-search at several universities and other scientific groups concerned with the connection between a person's facial features and their personality.

Facial and body type classification continues in modern popular psychology. For example, the personality type theory Socionics uses physiognomy in its personality type descriptions, and subjects such as NLP (Neuro Linguistic Programming) make common reference to body types and eye movements, together with language styles, in order to categorize a person's way of thinking.

Face reading is based on more than 3,000 years of observation and research that suggests there is an accurate correlation between the features of the human face and the personality traits of its owner.

Chapter 2
LEARNING TO READ FACES

"Everything is in the face." ~ *Cicero*

Face reading is a basic part of human nature. Before there was a spoken language, early humans had to rely on nonverbal communication. For early man, survival depended on the ability to interpret the meaning in the faces and body language of others. Today we intuitively read faces and body language, even if it is just to recognize each other, and most of us also develop an immediate impression of each person we meet.

One of the first things a new face reader will notice is that faces are not symmetrical. Most faces are, in fact, asymmetrical. For example, if an imaginary vertical line is drawn down the center of the face from the forehead to the chin, it is easy to notice all the differences between the left side of the face and right side of the face.

Everything has meaning in reading a face, including the differences in lines, eyebrows, eyes, the size of the nose, nostril shape, and ears. The more noticeable the difference, the more significant the meaning becomes. A face reader is always looking for extremes (sometimes referred to as *verys*) in proportion to the whole face.

Scientists have discovered that the left half of our brain controls the right side of our body, including everything on the right side of our face. The right side of the brain controls the left side of our body. It makes no difference whether you are right or left handed.

Functions of the left brain can be described as dividing the world into bits of information, which are organized into a logical chain to predict a satisfactory outcome. The left brain is all about logic, information, and factual and linear thinking. These left brain characteristics are reflected on the right side of the face. In other words, the right side of a person's face reflects how they take themselves into their outside world. It is their "public" face.

The right-brain functions can be described as a person's imaginative, intuitive, emotional, and dream world, which is reflected on the left side of the face. The left side of a person's face reflects their inner world. It is their "personal" face.

The asymmetrical face shows that a person has one style in their personal life and a different style in their public life. For example, a difference in eyebrow shape will show a different approach to personal life versus the public world. If the left eyebrow is arched or angled and right eyebrow is straight, this person wants to be in control of their personal affairs and relationships but not their business or public world. Every difference between the left and right sides of the face tells how a person handles things differently in their public life versus their personal life.

Below are three photographs showing the difference between the right and left sides of this person's face. The first photo is a composite of the right side, or public side, of the face (two right halves). The second photo shows a normal view of the face. The third photo is a composite of the left, or personal side, of the face (two left halves).

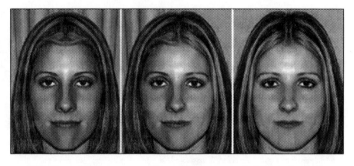

Right Face – Public   Normal Face   Left Face – Personal

As a face reader studies a person's face and reads each feature, they are always looking for verys and keeping in mind which side of the face they are analyzing to get a more clear-cut insight into the complete person.

WHERE DO A PERSON'S FEATURES COME FROM?

While it is true that a person's physical appearance is genetically based, researchers have discovered that people's personalities and character traits also have a genetic basis. People inherit facial features and many personality traits from their parents. A person's total personality is a combination of both nature and nurture. Genetics play an important part in the formation of a person's face, but it is not the only factor. On the nurture side, people's faces are affected by key events in their lives. Often when someone has experienced an intense loss or trauma, new lines will appear on their face. These lines can appear very quickly and become a permanent record of a specific life experience.

For example, one has only to notice the dramatic changes in the faces of many American presidents before they were elected and after only two or three years of occupying the oval office. The challenges of political life, while not easy, are nothing compared to the responsibilities of the Presidency. To a face reader it is striking that the faces of several recent presidents changed more than the faces of those who served around them during the same period of time.

Before some past presidents entered office they had cheeks that appeared tighter and more muscular. After two or three years in office their cheek padding increased significantly and their jowls became looser. These changes point toward a transformation of personal power from self-confidence to becoming less self-possessed. The jowls became flaccid indicating a symbol of decreased support from those around them and frustration over reduced control—resulting in more compromise.

Their lip proportions changed considerably during this period of their life. Before taking office many of these same presidents had a very full lower lip, indicating a gift for speaking and easy persuasiveness. After a couple of years the lower lip became notably thinner, meaning the way they communicated before had lost its impact and their speech had become a matter of finding a middle ground instead of their prior style of persuasive personal communication.

Mouth angle is another area that changed dramatically on many past presidents. While campaigning for the presidency, most candidates demonstrated a smile they hoped would suggest inner warmth and concern for the electorate. After a very short time in office the professional smile was still there, but the corners of the mouth began to turn down, indicating an expectation of problems and a mistrust of what others tell them.

Chapter 3
READING FACIAL FEATURES

"I have never been aware before how many faces there are. There are quantities of human beings, but there are many more faces, for each person has several."
~ Rainer Maria Rilke, Notebooks of Malte Laurids Brigge

In face reading, it is essential to become aware of how light reflects off a person's face. The way a face reflects light tells a lot about the person's inner character, and the way each facial feature responds to light points out the importance of that particular feature. Remember to look for verys, or extremes, that stand out or hide from the light.

According to physiognomist Mac Fulfer, J.D., facial features can have many meanings at the same time. For example, on the physical level, the nose is how we breathe, which we must do to survive. The nose is also a symbol for how we support ourselves. In other words, the nose reflects a person's work style and how they give and receive help to sustain and provide for themselves and others. Someone who has a very big nose that reflects a lot of light is a sign of a person who has a strong need to make a big impression on their outer world or who sees themselves as a provider and protector. The nose also shows how a person deals with money.

Another example of response to light is a heavy brow ridge on the forehead. In face reading, the forehead reflects a person's problem solving style. A heavy brow ridge on a forehead is like the bill of a baseball cap shading this person from light. If someone has this feature, they generally want to know how to do things using the proper procedure or by the rule. They have little use for approaches that do not produce a rule or procedure based plan of action.

Eyes that bulge out into the light signify that this person needs to be included. They love to talk and participate in conversation at every opportunity and their feelings may be hurt if they're interrupted or not included. They usually have much to contribute.

Someone with very deep-set out of the light eyes has a tendency toward protecting or guarding themselves, as if backed into a cavern. The person with this feature may look relaxed and at ease, but they are constantly analyzing their external world to keep their inner world safe.

In face reading, personal power is reflected in a person's cheeks. If a person possesses light-reflecting, high cheeks, seen on many celebrities, they will get attention as soon as they walk into a room. Their prominent cheeks signal their arrival for everyone to notice. They may also experience an occasional uncooperative or even jealous attitude toward them from others. It is not uncommon for people to overreact to these symbols of personal power.

A final example is the chin, the facial feature that reflects someone's level of assertiveness. A person who has a large chin or one that sticks out into the light tends to be more assertive and competitive. On the other hand, a person's whose chin is very receding and out of the light seldom projects hostility or competition and usually prefers a give-and-take attitude toward assertive behavior.

When the significance of a facial feature is fully understood, a face reader can gain insight into that feature's importance simply by paying attention to how it reflects light or hides from light.

On the following pages, variations of facial features are illustrated along with explanations of each feature's meaning, as well as some ideas to help you remember what they are.

FACE READING AT A GLANCE

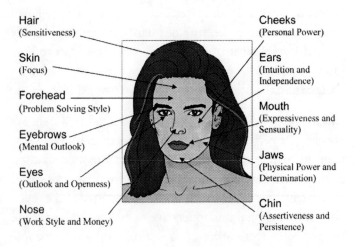

Hair
(Sensitiveness)

Skin
(Focus)

Forehead
(Problem Solving Style)

Eyebrows
(Mental Outlook)

Eyes
(Outlook and Openness)

Nose
(Work Style and Money)

Cheeks
(Personal Power)

Ears
(Intuition and Independence)

Mouth
(Expressiveness and Sensuality)

Jaws
(Physical Power and Determination)

Chin
(Assertiveness and Persistence)

Chapter 4
THE PERFECT FACE

*"I know not what beauty is, but I know
that it touches many things." ~ Dürer*

What is the perfect or beautiful face? Is beauty only in what each of us perceives, or are there some absolute values for it? It is said that beauty is in the eye of the beholder and that beauty varies by race, culture, or era. The evidence, however, shows that our perception of physical beauty is hardwired into our brains and based entirely on how closely one's features reflect Phi (a mathematical expression of an irrational number) in their proportions. Take another look at beauty through the eyes of mathematical science.

Phi is a Golden Number expressed as 1.61803398874989, or 1.618. It appears that everything in the universe is based on the proportion 1 to 0.618, which is commonly called the Golden Ratio.

A template for human beauty is found in this ratio. If we study the beauty of nature or art, we discover a common thread running through it. This common principle is the universal recognition of pleasing proportion. We all have a natural understanding of good proportion, and we agree that a work of art has good or bad proportion, or that a face looks too long, or too wide and out of proportion. This magical connecting thread of proportion known since ancient times as the Golden Ratio is very obvious when we look at human beauty.

The Concept

While the concept of the Golden Ratio is easy to understand, attempts to apply it can be complex and difficult to explain. Proportion usually means a relationship between a larger and a smaller. To make the concept clearer, the figure below shows several pairs of lines of different lengths and their ratio to each other. The last line shows the ratio of 1 to 0.618, which is the simplest form of the Golden Ratio.

The human face is based entirely on the Golden Ratio.

Dr. Stephen Marquardt, maxillo-facial surgeon, developed a beauty mask overlay based on the Golden Ratio. If an individual's face conforms to the beauty mask, then the face will be considered beautiful. There is a beauty mask for males and females based on the Golden Ratio, regardless of their race or culture. Dr. Marquardt performed cross-cultural surveys on beauty and found that all groups had the same perceptions of facial beauty. He also analyzed the human face from ancient times to the modern day. Through his research, he discovered that beauty is not only related to the Golden Ratio, but can be defined for both genders and for all races, cultures, and eras with the beauty mask that he developed and patented. This mask uses the pentagon and decagon as its foundation, which embody Phi in all their dimensions.

The Marquardt perfect beauty mask works best on faces that are fourteen to twenty-four years old, for humans are their most attractive two times in their lives: when they are infants (for survival) and when they are between the ages of fourteen and twenty-four (for attracting a mate).

Harry Perdew, Ph.D.

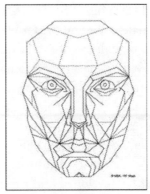

The Marquardt Mask

Asian   Black   Caucasian

1350 B.C. Egypt   500 B.C. Greece   164 A.D. Rome   1794 A.D.

*"There is no excellent beauty that hath
not some strangeness in the proportion."*
~ Francis Bacon

There are several facial features that excite aesthetic admiration, attraction, desire, or love. Although facial beauty is in the eye of the beholder, some features and their proportions are universally valued.

Researchers have found that there are several specific "beautiful" features in the face that are favored by humans in every society. Some of these features are wide-set eyes; full lips; and soft, smooth, and unblemished skin, all of which are attractive in both male and female faces. This response has evolved from the reaction of adults to the facial features of infants.

Across cultures, high cheekbones, a thin lower jaw, large eyes, a shorter distance between the mouth and chin and between the nose and mouth are preferred as "beautiful" qualities in men's and women's faces alike.

A research team in London found that eye contact with a pretty face—one that radiates empathy, cheerfulness, motherliness, and conventional beauty—activates a pleasure center in the brain called the ventral striatum. In men, female beauty stimulates the same pleasure centers of the brain as those stimulated by food and cocaine. They also found that this pleasure response, which appears in a matter of seconds after seeing the face, only happens when there is mutual eye-contact.

In a study utilizing Asian, Hispanic and white judges, the most attractive female faces had larger, wider-set eyes; smaller noses; narrower facial breadths; smaller chins; higher eyebrows; larger lower lips; larger smiles; dilated pupils; and well groomed, fuller hair.

Studies also show that when we scan someone's face we make repeated rest stops at the lips and eyes. When a face is viewed from the side, our eyes linger on the profiled nose, eye, ear, and lips.

The perfect face, male or female, is considered the "average" face. Face reading suggests that people with moderately proportioned (no verys) facial features are twice as fortunate. Besides being beautiful, these folks are relatively easy for others to understand and tend to gain greater social status because of their looks. However, when it comes to more innovative forms of talent, people who don't possess an average face tend to standout more often. For example, a face reader will see many verys or extremes by simply taking a look at the faces of American Presidents, none of whom have been endowed with an average face. In other words, while comparatively beautiful people may have social advantages, comparatively unattractive people stand a better chance for greatness.

RECOGNITION

As early as twelve weeks of age an unborn baby's face is recognizable in the womb. Although the face changes size and shape throughout the life cycle, it is nearly always recognizable to friends and family.

Face recognition is the awareness of having seen, met, known, or known of other people by recalling distinctive features of their faces. Our facial identification defines who we really are. The ability to recognize and recall thousands of faces easily and at a glance is a unique talent possessed by humans alone. Facial recognition is an active process, leading us to see faces in clouds and rock formations, in shrouds and on the surface of the moon. The ability to recognize faces lies in the brain's visual cortex, located at the back of the head on the occipital lobe. Interestingly, each face is stored in the brain in caricature.

COSMETIC SURGERY

Cosmetic surgery was first practiced in India more than a thousand years ago. Today plastic surgeons perform miracles that repair deformities and disfigurements resulting from congenital defects, wars, and accidents. Recently there has been an increase in the number of people seeking the help of cosmetic surgery to improve or change their facial appearance. The most common surgeries are on the nose, chin, ears and eyes, and the shape of the face, which affects other facial features.

According to physiognomist Rose Rosetree, having cosmetic surgery will not only change a person's features, but will also alter their personalities. In other words, the inner self will change with the new outer self. If the inner self does not change with the altered feature, the surgery will be unsuccessful. Even when the surgery is outwardly successful, adjusting to the facial change involves enormous inner chaos. When people are unwilling to change on the inside, the surgery does not work on the outside and the face will try to revert to its original configuration.

Here are some examples of what happens when someone has a facial feature altered by cosmetic surgery.

A nose profile that is aquiline or convex (page 65) made straight. After the surgical change, this person is less concerned about how they work. Previously this person could not get involved in a job unless they could do it creatively. What is lost is their gift for creative problem solving. Now they follow procedures without adding the individual spark they had before the facial change.

Ears that stick out (page 81) changed to ears that don't angle out. After surgery this person will fit in better socially, but some of the distinctive traits about their personality will be lost, such as their entrepreneurial spirit. They will begin to conform and take orders from others in their life, possibly causing long-term resentment and communication difficulties.

Very visible (heavy) upper lids (page 56) changed to small eyelid thickness. After surgery this person has increased self-esteem and seems more youthful. This facial change will create an obstacle to their feelings of intimacy with others, and they will have a feeling of being cut off from others without knowing why.

When studying faces, it is important for the face reader to look at the whole face, its shape and structure, and not rely on the reading of a single feature to the exclusion of all others. For example, in assessing a person's nose for such characteristics as power, creativity, and logic, the face reader may notice something inconsistent and suspect cosmetic surgery. Those findings should be checked by reading other parts of the face, which will confirm or deny the initial analysis.

Chapter 5
THE 60 SECOND READ

"It is the common wonder of all men, how among so many millions of faces, there should be none alike." ~ Thomas Browne, Religio Medici

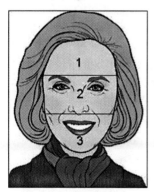

It is possible to actually get a quick read—within 60 seconds—of someone's face by looking at their facial dominance. A face can be divided horizontally into three zones to show dominant areas; Zone 1 from the top of the eyebrows to the original hairline, Zone 2 from the top of the eyebrows to the bottom of the nose, and Zone 3 from the bottom of the nose to the bottom of the chin. When one of these zones is more prevalent than the other two you have a quick clue to this person's related personality traits.

Large Zone 1

The person with a large Zone 1, where the area between the eyebrows and hairline is larger than the other two zones, focuses on thinking. These people enjoy the world of ideas, and want to acquire knowledge, especially in areas of personal interest. They like complete explanations with all the details. This person thinks everything through and makes decisions based on doing so. Feelings and emotions don't play much of a role in their thinking processes.

Small Zone 1

People with a small Zone 1, where the forehead is smaller than the other two zones, can be very determined, persistent, and intense. Not easily deterred, once they decide on a goal they will let nothing stand in the way of their obtaining it. These folks tend to be direct and less subtle. Their strength is to go after what they want no matter what gets in their way.

Large Zone 2

People with a large Zone 2, where the area between the eyebrows and the bottom of the nose is larger than the other two zones, tend to focus on money, status, luxury, and quality. They may also be ambitious, going into action to reach their goals and dreams, but their secret desire is to be envied by everyone for their success. These are people who are driven by their feelings and emotions. They make decisions based on whether something feels right. They enjoy the status of owning the best material things.

Small Zone 2

People with a small Zone 2, where the middle of the face is smaller than the other two zones, work hard for everything and always give more than one hundred percent. Their challenge is receiving the financial reward they deserve for their efforts and not being taken for granted. While they may not get rich, they will always be well-respected. It doesn't mean they can't gain wealth, just that they will work harder for it than someone with a larger Zone 2.

Large Zone 3

The person with a large Zone 3, where the area between the bottom of the nose and the bottom of the chin is larger than the other two zones, is well grounded and views life in a physical way. They have a good sense of themselves and their physical surroundings. When they say something will work, they've already checked to make sure it will. When they have a problem or need to make a decision, they do their best thinking when they can do something physical.

Small Zone 3

A person with a small Zone 3, where the area from the bottom of the nose to the bottom of the chin is smaller than the other two zones, is more connected to their inner world than their outer world. They are extremely sensitive and criticism can wound them. Their challenge is with the physical world. They may occasionally bump into things and often forget people's names soon after they've met them.

Chapter 6
Facial Coloring

"A face is like the outside of a house, and most faces, like most houses, give us an idea of what we can expect to find inside."
~ Loretta Young

Facial coloring indicates person's lifestyle preference. This facial feature determines if people need variety in their life or if they tend to be more conservative. Color refers to hair, eyebrows, eye color, and skin tone. People are divided into two types: light colored and dark colored.

Light Colored

To determine if a person has light coloring, look for a skin tone that is white with a tinge of yellow, ivory, or pink. Their hair color is white, silver, platinum, yellow, light brown, or a shade of red. Eyebrows are the same color as the hair. Finally, they might have eyes that are blue, green, gray, or light hazel. If a person has two of the three main characteristics, they are considered light-colored. These traits are common in people from northern latitudes where the skin is more sensitive to the elements and sunburn. Light-colored people tend to live in a more unstructured manner. These folks are more open-minded, less focused and love variety.

Dark Colored

People who are considered dark-colored have skin in shades of olive, gold, yellow, brown, dark gray, or black. Their hair color is a shade of dark brown, dark gray, or black. The eyebrows are the same color as the hair. Finally, their eyes are the color of dark hazel, brown, violet, or black. If a person has two of the three main characteristics, they are classified as dark colored. These traits are common in people from warmer climates where skin is less fair, less sensitive to the elements, and not as susceptible to sunburn. These folks carry on in a more conservative manner. They are not as spontaneous as the light-colored person. They tend to be serious minded, more focused, and don't thrive on variety.

Sometimes it is possible for light-colored people to have dark-colored characteristics and vice versa. For example, a dark-colored person may have blue eyes or a light-colored person could have brown eyes, resulting in a diminishing of those traits.

Chapter 7
HAIR AND SKIN

"A man finds room in the few square inches of his face for the traits of all his ancestors; for the expression of all his history, and his wants." ~ *Ralph Waldo Emerson, Conduct of Life*

The texture of the hair and skin determines how sensitive an individual is to sound, touch, taste and feelings. The finer the hair and skin, the greater the person's sensitivity; the coarser the hair and skin, the longer it takes for situations to annoy them.

Fine Hair and Skin

People with fine hair and skin tend to be hypersensitive. Their feelings are easily hurt and they are very vulnerable to loud noises or anything that is forceful and unpleasant. Fine-hair-and-skin folks prefer quality rather than quantity. They have a great deal of pride, high standards, and are apt to be less emotional. Their tastes lean towards idealism, and they can be critical or snobbish. They are more interested in how others conduct themselves, instead of how they look.

Coarse Hair and Skin

A person with coarse hair and skin that is freckled, bumpy, scarred, or wrinkled may appear to be less sensitive. They have feelings but they don't surface as quickly as the fine-hair-and-skin person. These folks enjoy things on a grand scale—loud music, a lot of food, boisterous laughter, and lots of intensity. They are more down to earth and practical. They can be the center of attention at social gatherings. They tend to be very approachable, and can be frank, bold, and forceful.

Combination Hair and Skin

Those people with a wide range of hair and skin textures may find themselves going back and forth in their moods. They may enjoy loud music at one moment, and find the noise unbearable at another time. They can show the traits of both fine- and coarse-textured hair and skin people.

Facial Hair

A face reader can pick up more clues to a person's personality when there's facial hair than when there's none. Facial hair is about sensitivity. It either hides or expresses a sensitive personality.

Mustaches

A person who wears a mustache feels the need to appear stronger than they really are, or in many cases men want to feel manlier. The fuller the mustache, the more the person needs to cover insecurity that comes with the fear of not being respected. If the mustache covers the upper lip, the person is not interested in divulging his innermost thoughts and feelings to someone else. If the upper lip is visible, the person is more apt to share those private thoughts.

Beards

Beards are an extension of the chin and make a person look and feel more masculine. Like people with a large Zone 3, the length of the beard extends the bottom third of the face. The bottom third is related to the nature of the physical. A longer beard would indicate that the person is more in touch with the physical world than with emotion or logic.

People with rounded beards are very people oriented, just like the person with a rounded chin. These folks have a genuine empathy and compassion for others. They may be trying to cover up their soft side with a rough beard so others won't take advantage of them.

A person with a squared beard likes to keep a focus on ideas and principles. These folks can be very assertive and demand to be taken seriously. Like a person with a square chin, they usually have a cause and are dedicated to accomplishing tasks.

Those people that have pointed beards are goal-directed people. They let nothing stand in the way of reaching their objectives. Similar to the pointed chin, these folks have a strong need to feel and be in control. These individuals like to do things their way and don't like to be wrong.

Bangs and hairstyles that cover or leave open the forehead

Similar to those folks with a mustache, people with bangs or hair styles that cover their forehead are less likely to talk about their private, personal, or business issues. They are not apt to discuss topics they believe are too personal or might be taboo.

The person who pulls their hair straight back and exposes their entire forehead is more likely to talk freely about anything others may want to know. Their thoughts are open and ready to be shared with the world.

Chapter 8
THE FOREHEAD

"The serial number of a human specimen is the face, that accidental and unrepeatable combination of features." ~ Milan Kundera

The shape of the forehead can indicate a great deal about a person's thought processes, problem solving style, self-esteem, memory, and hidden behaviors.

Round and Full

A round, full forehead indicates a desire to use imagination and originality in problem solving. These folks are quick thinkers who respond in the moment. They are inclined to let their past experiences determine their decision making. They tend to deal more with the reaction to challenges than the challenge itself. They have great memories and retain much of what they hear.

Slopes Back

This type of forehead indicates a strong development of memory and quick mental reactions. These people appreciate applications of proven methods and procedures to avoid wasting time. Everything they do—like talking, thinking, reading, and decision making—is done quickly. Once they've seen something done, they can often remember exactly how to do it easily.

Flat

People with a flat forehead think sequentially, step-by-step, and have trouble understanding information that is presented too fast or out of sequence. They need time to assimilate things and, as a consequence, don't think well under pressure. They tend to deal more with the challenge than with the reaction to the challenge. Their strength is that, when they learn something, they retain it for life.

Wide

A person with a forehead that appears wider than average above the ears has a forehead that would be considered wide. A wide forehead indicates a gift for dominating others and leading. These folks tend to have large egos and protect themselves from showing any signs of weakness. They are idealists with a wealth of ideas. They are very courageous, unafraid of unfamiliar situations, and are at ease when taking full responsibility for others.

Narrow

People with foreheads that are narrower than average above the ears tend to stick with their ideas, jobs, and opinions to a degree of possible stubbornness. They are usually creatures of habit and resent change. They are not as brave as the person with a wide forehead, especially in unpleasant situations. These folks are ambitious, persistent, and patient but have no interest in leadership positions. They handle details well and may be experts in their chosen field.

High

People with high foreheads tend to have high standards and ideals. They have good memories and are skilled in human relations. They like to think things through and don't always do well in social situations. These folks enjoy the world of ideas, and want to learn more, especially about things that interest them. They want all the details. They like abstract ideas, imagination, and theories. They are usually cordial and polite, and are not easily convinced.

Low

Those folks whose forehead is low can be very determined, persistent, and intense. Not easily deterred, once they decide on a goal, they will let nothing stand in the way of their obtaining it. Their strength is to go after what they want no matter what gets in their way. They can be self-centered and egotistical. They tend to be intelligent, shrewd and, outspoken—even on issues they know nothing about.

Brow Ridge

People that have a well-defined ridge that divides the brow from the forehead are very matter of fact and rules-and-procedure oriented. They do things according to the rules. Once the rules are understood and accepted, these folks will follow them to the letter and expect others to do the same. They don't like change and tend to be very conservative by nature.

Pressure Point Pads

People with pressure point pads, bulges on each side of the forehead just above the eyebrows, have very good imaginations. They are able to create mental images and ideas easily. These folks also have a high degree of neatness and organization. They set very high standards and resent anything that does not meet these standards.

Chapter 9
EYEBROWS

"Everyone wants to pluck eyebrows. I thinned them out real thin once and it just didn't look like me." ~ Denise Richards

The eyebrow personalizes people perhaps more than any other feature that is read. The shapes of the eyebrows are powerful visual cues that can create a response in others. There are three basic shapes of eyebrows: straight, which look like a straight line; curved, which form part of a circle; and arched or angled, which contain an apex where the hair changes direction. Each shape denotes a different mental outlook. The placement of the eyebrow, high or low in relationship to the eye, indicates whether a person is more selective and formal or friendly and casual.

Shape

Straight

Those people with straight eyebrows are direct and want the facts and all the details. They make decisions based on logic and need to be shown all the facts before accepting something as true. They generally don't let emotions affect their way of thinking. They are consistent and well-balanced in their emotions and behavior. Their approach is logical, direct, and factual. They tend to have an enlarged visual appreciation of the world around them.

Curved

Folks who are endowed with curved eyebrows are people oriented. They connect with the world best through their understanding of people. They prefer not to be burdened with too many details without seeing a real-world application. They are generally very receptive to all types of people; they are good listeners and are open to other's opinions and ideas. They are good organizers and have the ability to bring things together.

Arched

For the person with arched or angled eyebrows, there is the need to stay mentally in control of any situation in which they find themselves. Outgoing and open, they may have good leadership qualities because of their ability to be detached. They are imaginative, clever with words, and hate to be wrong. They have the ability to see the big picture of whatever interests them.

DISTANCE BETWEEN EYE AND EYEBROW

The relative distance between the eyebrows and the eyes gives information about how a person puts their thoughts out into the world.

Lowbrow

Someone with eyebrows that are close to their eyes has the tendency to be expressive, quick to take action, and may interrupt others to express themselves, because if they don't say it now, it may not get said. They are mentally quick and spontaneous communicators. These folks are more affable and make friends easily. They make decisions based on logic rather than feelings.

Highbrow

People with eyebrows with more space between the eye and the eyebrow tend to be perceptive, selective, and discriminating. They have a wait-and-see attitude and need time to assimilate new information before acting. They are not apt to speak without thinking first. It is very important for these folks to know how they feel about a topic and how all the parts relate to the whole. They make decisions based on feelings rather than logic.

Middlebrow

A person with middlebrows is flexible. In certain situations they will practice beforehand and in other situations they will tell it like it is. They are not apt to blurt out information like a lowbrow or appear as guarded as the highbrow. These folks make decisions based on a combination of logic and feelings.

EYEBROW VARIATIONS

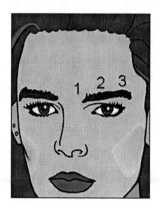

Hair Distribution

The distribution of hair on eyebrows is important to the face reader because it tells how a person works with details. The best way to analyze hair distribution is to divide each eyebrow into three areas. Area 1 is the hair that grows on the inside, nearest the nose and the middle of the face. Area 2 is the middle third of the eyebrow, and Area 3 represents the outside third, closest to the ear.

Starters

With the starter eyebrows (Area 1), hair begins close to the nose and is strong at the start, then fades into areas 2 and 3. By the end of the eyebrow, there is little or no hair. These folks have a talent for new projects and ideas, but their interest wanes quickly as new ideas come to mind. If the hair ends halfway (Area 2) across the eyebrow, they will lose interest half way through the project.

Enders

Those who have ender eyebrows (Area 3) have difficulty starting projects but are great at details and finishing tasks. Once these folks begin a project, they will generally see it through to the end. They have a talent for following up on details, and the further they get into a project the more details they can find to fix. These people tend to be perfectionists.

Eveners

People with even eyebrows through all three areas generally start and finish projects. Their thought process flows smoothly. They get an idea, develop it, and work out all the necessary details. Their enthusiasm and interest levels are consistent from beginning to end. They tend to get frustrated with folks who aren't as adept at handling details as they are.

Unibrow

People with one solid growth of hair from one side of the face to the other, filling all six areas and between the eyes, are nonstop thinkers. Sometimes the thinking is so intense that they have difficulty relaxing or falling to sleep. These folks are usually male because women generally pluck or shave this hair from between their eyebrows. Plucking or shaving the hair between the eyebrows will cure the sleepless nights and an overactive brain.

Startup Hairs

Startup or access hairs are hairs growing straight up at the beginning of the eyebrow (Area 1), in contrast to the rest of eyebrow hair, which tends to grow sideways. These special hairs indicate a person has a strong connection between their inner feelings and their logical thinking. They tend to be immediately aware of potential problems within their world. These folks are the first to recognize something might be risky or even dangerous.

Scattered Hairs

Scattered hairs in Area 3 reveal a person who is very curious and may ask a lot of questions. If their eyebrows are thin, they may be too self-conscious to actually ask the question. Because these folks have scattered thoughts on many different topics, each hair could be read as a separate interest. Sometimes they have trouble following up on their interests in a consistent manner.

Chameleon

The person with chameleon eyebrows, which are light in color almost blend into the brow, sometimes appears to have no eyebrows, but they do. This is a person who naturally blends in well with others. They can be in a room full of people and carry on a conversation with anyone in the room on almost any subject. Other people think they are just like them, even if they're not.

Tangled

People with tangled eyebrows have a penchant for attracting conflict with others. They love to challenge other people's knowledge about a certain subject just for the sake of seeing if there is anything that's been missed. They are unconventional thinkers whose thoughts range to many subjects.

Executive

A person with this set of unique eyebrows—thinner in Area 1 and thicker in Area 3—is usually very well organized. They may be slow cautious starters, but once a project is underway they are on board to its completion. They are noted for following through and can be depended upon to cover all the details.

THICK OR THIN

The amount of hair in a set of eyebrows shows how much detail people feel comfortable handling, in other words, how many balls they can keep in the air at one time.

Thick

Thick or bushy eyebrows in-dicate someone who is men-tally active and has intellectual power. They are deep thinkers who can take a concept to new levels. These folks can juggle many projects at once, and if their eyebrows are even or enders, they are exceptionally good at keeping the details for each project under control.

Thin

A person with thin eyebrows is a very intense thinker. They push themselves to be multi-taskers, but are much more effective handling one project at a time. Because of this, they organize and execute around priorities. People with very thin eyebrows tend to be overly self-concious and sensitive. They need to be reassured.

It is important to look at both eyebrows carefully because the right and left eyebrows may not be the same. For example, a person may finish projects at work (right eyebrow) but not start or finish personal projects (left eyebrow).

A person's personality, as well as the way they perceive themselves and others, will change when they use make up or alter (such as plucking) any feature. The only exception is when someone is purposely trying to look like someone they are not, such as an actor.

Chapter 10
Eyes

"The eyes have one language everywhere." ~
George Herbert

Eyes represent a person's outlook on life, openness to others, emotional expression, stress level, and dishonesty. They are the features people look at first when meeting someone. Eyes can also tell when people filter or screen out information. The spacing, size, angle, and depth of each eye will tell a lot about how a person approaches life.

Eye Spacing

The first thing a face reader looks at when reading a person's eyes is spacing, that is, the distance between the eyes. The average spacing between a person's eyes is about one eye-width apart.

Wide

Those folks who have widely spaced eyes (more than one eye-width apart) tend to be broadminded and have an open perspective and a far-sighted imagination. These are big picture people who sometimes miss out on something important because they overlook details. They are very tolerant and more laid back when reacting to situations and tend to put up with a lot before responding.

Narrow

People who have closely spaced eyes (less than one eye-width apart) are very focused on details and excel at exacting tasks where minute details are important. They do well in positions that require extreme focus but often can't see the big picture and don't relate well to others on their terms. These folks tend to be biased and less tolerant of themselves and others.

Eye Size

The size of the iris, the colored part of the eye, reflects how much a person expressively responds to their surroundings.

Large

People with large, full irises connect with their feelings and are more prone to show and express what they are feeling. They also have a visual, hands-on approach and need to see the information they receive. They listen best when they are looking at the person talking or what the person speaking is talking about. These folks tend to be honest and trustworthy expecting the same from those around them.

Small

People with small irises tend to show little emotion and can be affected by other people's actions and point of view. These folks are motivated by physical expressions of encouragement and acceptance. They are always on guard against someone trying to deceive or trick them. They tend to make decisions with their head rather than with their emotions.

EMOTIONAL REACTIONS

A person's eyes are in a constantly moving with each upsetting feeling or thought. People's eyes react to indicate their actual mental state in the moment.

Stress

When people experience mental stress they have a corresponding physiological reaction: Their irises float up. This phenomenon is sometimes referred to as sanpaku. This response becomes visible as white showing between the lower eyelid and the iris of the eye. The larger the white area is, the more the stress they are feeling.

Rage

If a person's eyes show white above the iris, it is an indication not only of emotional stress, but also that the person may react in a violent manner. They may treat others with degradation and contempt. These folks may conceal an explosive temper, and this feature could also be an indication of mental imbalance.

Eye Angle

The angle of a person's eyes indicates their world view and perspective. The eye angle will indicate whether they are an optimist, pessimist, or realist. Each eye can have different angles, which may reflect conflicting views.

Angle Up

If the eyes angle up, the person is an optimist and demonstrates a great deal of inspiration and imagination. They focus on the positive things in life. They expect things to turn out for the best. These folks know how to get what they want. This mindset helps them accomplish things others would never try. They also have the ability to keep a secret.

Angle Down

People with eyes that angle down expect problems and, because they gain wisdom from the past, are especially good at spotting potential trouble. They may find that people come to them with their problems, because the angle of their eyes shows genuine compassion for the suffering of others. When they give you their word on something, they keep it.

Opposite Angles

People with opposite-angled eyes are capable of seeing things from a different perspective and applying creative thought processes to solving problems. These folks will analyze comments and observations with an out-of-the-box mentality. They often amaze others with the spur-of-the-moment insights that they offer.

Level

Those people whose eyes are not at an angle have a balanced view of life and tend to be pragmatic and objective. They are not easily discouraged and possess resilience under stress. They are concerned with fairness and evenhandedness in everything they do.

Eye Depth

The depth of the eye in the socket indicates a person's view about contributing in personal and public situations. The more out-front the eyes are, the more these folks will jump right in. The more recessed the eyes, the more guarded a person is.

Bulging

People with eyes that appear to bulge out of their sockets are naturally enthusiastic and eager to participate. They don't have to run the show, but they want to be included in everything that is happening. They tend to contribute many ideas to the projects in which they are involved. They love to talk and will feel hurt if interrupted. They may put up emotional barriers, feeling they are not appreciated. These folks are not always cautious about what they say and can easily tell all.

Recessed

Those people who have eyes that are recessed deep into their sockets appear to be calm and relaxed, but are in fact intense and possessive. They are continually evaluating everything. They question things carefully and need proof before accepting anything. They protect their inner self by being reserved, cautious, and observant. It's not easy to get them to talk, but when they are in the mood, they can be very effective speakers.

Eye Color

The color of the eye is important in determining a person's character and personality traits.

Blue-eyed people will tell someone exactly what's on their mind. They will express how they feel and consistently stand behind their opinions. The lighter the shade of blue, the stronger the trait. Deep blue eyes indicate a highly sensual and sensitive person. Light blue eyes belong to those people who are likely to be big flirts.

Green-eyed people enjoy having people around them more than being by themselves. Meeting and talking with new people is stimulating to them. They are spontaneous and sometimes a bit willful. They are very inventive in both practical and personal affairs. People with green eyes often display great genius.

Brown-eyed people tend to have a more pedagogical mentally. They are good at carrying out their plans and always give one hundred percent of themselves. These folks are constantly interested in improving themselves.

Hazel-eyed people are very considerate of other people's feelings. They have a built in caring quality, preferring to have everyone get along, and have a strong desire to be liked by others. These folks tend to be understanding, flexible, and accommodating.

Gray-eyed people tend to be more timid and dislike confrontations that can cause them any stress or anxiety. While they have a high degree of intellect and imagination, they are a lot less passionate about things. They tend to be shy, reserved, refined, and difficult to please.

Black-eyed people, while very rare, enjoy competition and will challenge anything and enjoy doing so. They do not give up under any circumstances. Occasionally, their eyes can appear to have a purple or violet radiance. These folks tend to be strong natured and not always tactful when interacting with others.

Eyelids

The eyelids are not only important for keeping dirt and dust out of the eyes; they also serve as an incredible source of communication. Upper eyelids reflect a person's intimacy requirements. Bottom lids are about wariness, suspicion, skepticism, shyness, or a judgmental attitude. They also indicate a person's vulnerability and trust.

Heavy

People with very visible or heavy upper lids have a strong need for intimacy. These folks bond with their partners and want to share all aspects of life with their significant other. They give and demand closeness and are emotionally generous toward others.

Thin

A person with thin upper eyelids has balanced intimacy needs in relationships. They welcome closeness but are also capable of acting independently. Because they need their own emotional space, these folks are unsympathetic to any kind of codependence.

Not Visible

People who have upper eyelids that are not visible when their eyes are open are endowed with the gift of focus and must have their own personal space. When they are focused on a task, they don't like demands placed upon them by others. These folks are capable of intimacy, but only when they are ready for it.

Harry Perdew, Ph.D.

Straight Bottom

Those folks who have straight bottom lids try to maintain an emotional distance or a self-protective stance. They are wary, suspicious, shy, and keep their guard up, making them tough to approach. Once they accept someone, however, they can be a most loyal friend and supporter.

Curved Bottom

Curved bottom lids indicate a person who is positive, receptive, and open to people and new ideas. They tend to be curious and are willing to take in information and gather all the facts that are available. Their lower lids become more curved when these folks are really listening to what someone is saying.

Very Curved Bottom

People with extremely rounded bottom lids are very open and usually emotionally vulnerable and trusting. They can also be very blunt and lacking in tact when dealing with others.

Eyelashes

Long

People whose eyelashes are long and full are tolerant, accepting, and usually have a gentle disposition. These folks tend to be sensual and optimistic. They are easy to get along with because they tend to keep everything around them in focus.

Short

Those folks that are endowed with thin and short eyelashes are extremely sensitive. They may get their feelings hurt easily and be quick to anger. They are less optimistic and physical than the person with longer eyelashes.

Eye Padding

Some people have loose skin above the eye that is called eye padding. Eye padding indicates a person's patience, sensitivity and criticalness.

Moderate

If a person has moderate eye padding, where the skin above the lids appears like an extra fold, they tend to focus so hard on their external environment that they sometimes forget about their own needs. In doing so, they become impatient, overly sensitive, critical, and downright disagreeable. These folks are especially analytical about other people.

Heavy

People with intense eye padding have a passion for high achievement, and are, for the most part, ill-natured, defensive, selfish, and sometimes deceitful. Having this attitude does not make this person happy, even when they try to convince others that they are. These folks tend to offer others advice that is sometimes perceived as criticism.

Chapter 11
THE NOSE

"Your whole personality is in your nose."
~ Edith Piaf

The nose is perhaps the most important feature on the face. The nose gives insights about how people support themselves and those around them. The nose not only indicates a person's vitality level, but it also reveals their work style and how they deal with money. The ideal nose has a high ridge, is straight with a full tip, and medium-flared nostrils that are hidden when viewed from the front.

SIZE AND SHAPE

Large

People with large noses have a great need to make a major contribution in their work. They are at their best when they are in charge, because they want to have a significant impact on their work. These folks are not satisfied with work when they feel their efforts don't make a big difference.

Small

People who have small noses tend to have less physical energy and strength. These folks do not like confrontations and will sacrifice as a result. However, they can stand their ground if it means their self-respect.

Long

A person with a long nose has the need and ability to control his or her work environment, including both the environment and the style of the work. They operate best in situations where they can control the tempo and priority of the work as well. These folks have a gift for long-range planning and strategy.

Short

People with a short nose like to get down to business and get the job done. They are not afraid of hard work and have an exceptional ability to handle the boring details that would be difficult for most people. Because these folks have a tendency to always give more than one hundred percent they tend to become workaholics.

Straight

People with long and straight noses are logical long-range planners and strategists. They lead the way in discovering new ideas and take a logical, no-nonsense approach to their work. These folks love check lists and emphasize procedures. Most of their decisions are based on logic.

Concave

Folks with concave noses allow feelings and emotions to have an important impact on their work. In a positive, supportive environment there is nothing they can't do, but in a stressful environment it is very difficult for them to accomplish anything. They must receive some kind of positive appreciation for their efforts to function at their best. They make decisions base on how they feel.

Convex

People with convex or aquiline noses appreciate beauty and elegance, but their real talent is in creative problem solving. They can usually see better ways to do things and are not afraid to try them. They are efficiency experts and are comfortable directing others. These folks are also very aware of costs versus value.

NOSE RIDGE

No Ridge

People who have no nose ridge are happiest when they can work with others. They enjoy working in teams where they can feel at one with and share knowledge. If they have to work alone, these folks may feel left out.

High

Those folks who have a high nose ridge would rather work by themselves and do best when they can control tempo of their work. They don't like anyone looking over their shoulder or kibitzing while they do their work.

Wide

The person with a high wide nose ridge has extraordinary willpower and strength of mind. They don't let anything stop them from getting what they go after. These folks can get what they want by sheer force of will.

NOSE WIDTH

On each side of the nose tip there is a rim that covers the nostrils. The width of a person's nose at its base is determined by the distance between the outside of their nostril rims. These rims indicate how people give and receive support from others.

Wide

The person with a wide nose at the bottom is very supportive and protective of loved ones and those close to them. They are able to accept support from others and willingly share with them. These folks also have an incredible gift for teamwork.

Narrow

People with narrow noses at the bottom have had to basically make it on their own. These folks tend to be independent and self-sufficient, taking care of their own needs. They find it very difficult to be on the receiving end of any type of emotional or physical support.

Nose Tip

The nose tip angle indicates a person's willingness to trust and shows whether they are skeptical, mistrustful, or accepting. It also shows their level of patience with others.

Turns Up

A person whose nose tips turns up tends to be a spur-of-the-moment person. They do well in social situations and enjoy mixing with other people. They are impetuous and impulsive, and may find it hard to keep a secret. They are open to others and ready to hear whatever story they are being told. These folks are not very patient.

Turns Up Pointed

People with a turned up nose and a pointed tip are very curious—especially about people. They find it very difficult to hold onto money and are apt to spend it freely. The more turned up the nose tip is, the less patience this person has.

Level

If a person has a nose that neither turns up or down, he or she tends to be very dependable and have a good business sense. They are able to trust others without being easily fooled. These folks tend to express a normal amount of patience.

Turns Down

Someone whose nose tip turns down tends to be mistrustful, cynical, cunning, and shrewd, even toward those who are closest to them. They only accept others after they have proven themselves. These folks show a great deal of patience, but when it wears thin, look out.

Turns Down Pointed

People who have nose tips that are turned down and pointed tend to be unfeeling, self-serving, and even deceitful. These folks have trouble figuring out how to be considerate and accepting of other people's viewpoints. To understand a person's attitude about financial security look at the tip of their nose.

Large Ball

People who have a very large nose tip are very interested in finding financial security, especially a steady stream of cash. These folks are always concerned about the scarcity of anything. They know a lot about how the money system works and use it to their advantage. They also tend to be collectors.

Small Ball

The person with a small ball at the tip of their nose appreciates art and beauty. They know quality when they see it and always look for the finest in everything they own. These folks have a very imaginative approach to life.

Pointed

People who have a pointed nose tip tend to be very curious about the world around them. They also instinctively want to help others improve their lives. Very often, this need to improve others is expressed in what may feel like criticism to the person on the receiving end.

Thin

Someone whose nose tip is thin and pinched has little concern with holding onto money and is apt to be a free spender. Money is only prized for what it can buy. Because these folks believe that there will always be enough money, saving or investing is just not their fashion.

Notched

People with a groove or notch in the tip of their nose are concerned with finding their calling in life. Their work must be emotionally satisfying to them, or they won't be truly happy until it is. These folks may have many jobs and careers before the find their own niche.

NOSTRILS

The size and shape of the nostrils gives indications about a person's vitality or flow of energy. Size and shape also goes along with how they spend or don't spend money.

Large

Folks with large nostrils have a bold, open approach to living and can be very daring. They are innovative and big-hearted to a fault. These folks have the potential to nurture others in a loving and caring manner. Spending money is not a problem for these people. In fact, they are passionate about it.

Small

People with very small nostrils know the value of money and are very unadventurous and frugal. They usually live with a fear of scarcity and think they never have enough. They are great savers. These folks have a tendency to avoid going into debt.

Long

Those that have long, narrow nostrils may be emotionally generous but, like their small nostrils relatives, are very tight with their money. These folks are ready to give others emotional support but are not as apt to give them financial assistance.

Flared

A person with huge, flared nostrils is self-confident and has a flair for extravagant spending. Their energy is so intense that they may overestimate their own abilities and tend go to extremes. These folks usually take on too much because they think they are unbeatable.

Round

People who have round nostrils are always willing to give and are bighearted to a fault with both their time and riches. Because they are satisfied with their own wealth and possessions, these folks share what they have with those who are near and dear to them.

Rectangular

Someone with rectangular-shaped nostrils is a conservative spender who takes pleasure in budgeting. These folks are fundamentally conservative in the way they spend time and money. They are not your big risk takers.

Triangular

Those folks who have small, tri-angular-shaped nostrils are financially conservative and may be miserly, holding on tightly to whatever they have. They have a fear of not having enough of something, which may or may not involve money. It could mean friends, love, time, or anything else that would give them a strong sense of security.

The Septum

The septum is located at the bottom of the nose between the nostrils. If this feature is long and hangs well below the nose flange, it indicates this person is someone who is very analytical by nature. These folks especially like to analyze other people. A short septum would indicate its owner is less analytical.

Harry Perdew, Ph.D.

The Philtrum

The vertical groove linking the nose to the upper lip is called the philtrum. People who have a well developed and defined philtrum are endowed with high energy and vitality levels. Conversely, people with a flat, undefined philtrum have a markedly reduced life force and get-up-and-go. The width and depth of the philtrum is also an indication of a person's interest in sex. The wider and deeper this feature is, the stronger the person's sex drive.

Chapter 12
Ears

"It's interesting, because I tend to trust a man with big ears." ~ Mo Rocca

The ears take information in from all directions at one time. The shape, size, and position of a person's ears reflects their individual reality. Ears are also a sign of how a person takes in and assimilates information and makes decisions, whether literally or intuitively.

Ear Size

Large

People who have large ears are always ready to listen to others. They assimilate information more slowly and carefully. Their responses may take longer because decisions are not made until enough information has been obtained. They like to mull over their thoughts before making a decision. These folks also tend to be caring, amenable, and giving.

Small

A person with small ears tends to focus on their own counsel and is less accepting of what they hear from others. They gather information easily and quickly. Information is processed as it is received. These folks are spontaneous and may jump to conclusions too soon, but they are usually quick-witted enough to recover gracefully.

Ear Helixes (Rims) and Ridges

Prominent Outer Rim

People with prominent outer ear rims tend to focus on the outside world. They enjoy working with objective data, figures, and statistics. These folks use a commonsense style that is both logical and practical. They require external proof and data before they can make a final decision.

Prominent Inner Ridge

People with prominent inner ear ridges focus on their internal world and thoughts. They have a creative, innate, and highly one-sided approach. Before they accept something as being true, it must pass their instinctive feelings. Being logical usually has nothing to do with it.

Clear Separation

Those folks who have a clear separation between the inner ridge and outer ear rims maintain a good balance between their private life and their work life. They think about things carefully before responding or acting.

No Separation

A person who has no clear definition between ridge and rim may overestimate their abilities and, at times, tend to be somewhat egotistical. These folks rely solely on their feelings to act, without considering the reality or consequences of their actions.

EAR PLACEMENT

Another aspect of the ear a face reader should look at is the angle of the ears or how they are placed on the head—the greater the angle the stronger the trait. Ear angle also relates to how people deal with social conventions.

Vertical

People with ears that are placed on a parallel angle with the head have an evenhanded awareness and perception. They are comfortable operating within what is expected of them and what is customary.

Angled

Individuals with ears placed at a distinct angle slanting backwards have a very specific point of view and outlook on life. These folks consistently see their environment from their own unique view of how the world works.

Stick Out

People who have ears that stick out are self-reliant non-conformists who tend to move ahead on their own. They are the original, out-of-the-box thinkers. These folks simply have their own set of rules and tend to follow them. They are quick thinkers with a stub-born streak and generally are not joiners.

Close to Head

The person whose ears are close to their head prefers to conform to accepted social standards. They are joiners who don't want to appear too dissimilar from others. These folks are generally conservative, know what is expected of them, prefer to follow procedure, and more often than not, aim to please.

EAR LOBES

Ear lobe size relates to a person's priorities about being metaphysical or physical.

Large

People with large ear lobes have a fascination with physical reality. Those with large and puffy ear lobes take life much too literally. These folks have good memories and are usually able to anticipate a major problem before it arises.

Small

Those people with small ear lobes relate more to a metaphysical orientation. They tend to be stubborn, and material comforts are more important to them than most other things in life. These folks can be a little on the impractical side.

Crease

A crease in the ear lobe comes from deep emotional and spiritual pain. The crease tracks the impact of deep stress, often having the emotional undertone of disillusionment. It can also be a signal of hypertension. These folks need to watch out for heart related problems.

EAR SHAPE

Rounded

The person who has a rounded outer edge to their ear has great sensitivity to sound and rhythm. The more rounded the ear the greater accuracy and reception of sound a person has. If this person has a completely round inner ear rim (helix) they tend to have good pitch, especially if the ear is cupped.

Straight

People who have ears that have a straight outer helix have an innovative trait. They like new ideas and being on the leading edge of anything new. Some of these folks are visionaries who want to be first to venture into a new field. They dislike working for someone else because of their independent spirit. Pointy ears mean that their owner is not as kind-hearted or reliable as they appear.

Ear Height

High

People with high tops (even or higher than the eye) tend to absorb information immediately. These folks approach life with a "let's do it now" mentality. They are more interested in seeing results. Doing something right is not as important as getting it done now. Sometimes this characteristic causes them to overlook important details.

Low

The folks with low bottoms (lower than bottom of the nose) have a "lets do it right" methodology. Being a patient listener, they feel they will miss something if they are forced to hurry. These individuals are always ready to hear more.

Chapter 13

CHEEKS

"It's the chubby cheeks. The whole reason people voted for me on American Idol is because I'm an everyday, normal girl." ~ Kelly Clarkson

Cheeks indicate a person's personal and leadership power as perceived by others. Often the first response people receive from others is their unconscious response to their cheeks.

High

People with high, protruding cheeks, commonly called high cheek bones, instantly get attention when they enter a room. They are perceived as a strong person even if they themselves don't believe they are. These folks love publicity and consistently exhibit a great deal of personal power. The individual with this feature tends to be more comfortable leading than following.

Full

Those folks that endowed with full cheeks that are rounded with no bones showing are non-threatening and convey an acceptance and tolerance of others. They are able to get people to support their causes. They have no trouble organizing a group or getting consensus whenever they need it.

Narrow

A person with narrow cheeks has powerful bursts of energy, but they need to take occasional periods of rest to become refreshed. These folks dislike situations that just plod along and work best when they can take occasional breaks. Slower people tend to drive them to distraction.

Wide

People with wide cheeks persevere because they have a great deal of energy and endurance. They approach tasks with a "can do" attitude and incredible personal power. Rest is not in the picture for these folks. The person with this feature has a slower, steady never-quit attitude.

Sunken

Those folks with sunken cheeks tend to lack personal strength and possibly suffer from physical illness or strained feelings. They are more focused on their internal world than on their outer world. Because these individuals tire easily, they need to continually conserve their energy.

Healer

Some people have what are called healer cheeks. These folks have an aura of encouraging, healing, and inspirational power. They adapt to the health fields, education, and parenting. Their special gift is an ability to inspire and give confidence to others.

Chapter 14
The Mouth

"Watch the mouth; it reveals what the eyes try to hide." ~ John Thaw

The mouth brings people into the most direct contact with their environment. It points out their style of self-expression and how they interpret what others tell them. The mouth is also an indicator of a person's sensuality.

Mouth Size

Large

People with large mouths tend to be demonstrative, gregarious, and talkative. They show more confidence in expressing themselves, and the larger the mouth the more expressive they are. These folks tend to be very friendly and may say things they don't believe just to get along with the group.

Small

Those folks with small mouths tend to be more reticent and reserved. They are cautious and don't reveal their inner thoughts and feelings until they know someone very well. They are sincere and choose their words more for truth than popularity.

Mouth Angle

Mouth angle reflects how people listen to what is being said.

Up Turned

A person with an upturned mouth is an optimistic listener. They always hear only the best in what others tell them. These folks expect to be praised by others.

Straight

People whose mouths are straight are unbiased listeners. They have the ability to realistically reflect back to a speaker what that someone has said. These folks neither expect praise nor criticism from others.

Down Turned

Those people with mouths that turn down tend to mistrust what others tell them. They generally don't have high expectations so are not disappointed when things don't turn out the way they hoped. They don't look for praise from others. These folks tend to be kind to people, not wanting to hurt anyone's feelings.

Lips

The lips are the part of the mouth that form the words people speak and the kisses people give one another. The upper lip represents feminine energy and aspects of an individual's inner world, including their feelings. The lower lip signifies a person's masculine energy, showing how people relate to their external world and get things done.

SIZE AND SHAPE

Full

People with full upper and lower lips are emotionally expressive and sensuous and may be physically affectionate. They have a good sense of humor and enjoy expressing themselves. These folks do have a tendency to talk about personal matters, sometimes telling more than others need or want to know.

Full Lower

The person with a full lower lip has the ability to convince others of their point of view. They are especially influential about the external world of facts and figures. They are endowed with a natural gift of persuasion. These folks can easily charm others no matter what they are discussing.

Full Upper

People with a full upper lip are candid and straight forward. These folks have a strong radar system that quickly detects deception in others. They are very articulate and enjoy expressing themselves. They also have the uncanny ability to know what's happening behind closed doors.

Thin

Those people with very thin lips tend to be reserved and cautious. They don't trust easily. They especially mistrust adulation and verbal expressions of emotion. They are very careful not to say anything that would expose them to criticism. These folks tend to stifle themselves and rarely talk about personal feelings.

Teeth

In face reading, people's teeth show how they make decisions and give indications of personal strength and resolve. Teeth symbolize the ability to break down life experiences, analyze them, and make choices. Front teeth also denote the size of a person's ego and their level of stubbornness.

Even

People with even teeth have a logical approach and seem to learn life's lessons quickly. They make decisions with assurance and self-confidence. These folks have an exceptional inner balance, and they get along well with everyone.

Crooked

Those people who have crooked teeth, especially bottom teeth, see both sides of every issue. Holding themselves to impossibly high standards, they hate to be wrong so they often double check their facts before proceeding. Because they see both sides of a situation, they sometimes have trouble making a choice between the two.

Gap

A person with a gap between their front teeth is willing to take chances even when they're not sure of the results. They tend to make decisions in the moment, based on intuition. Because they don't often have a clear sense of direction, they have a habit of changing their minds. The larger the gap is between the teeth, the stronger the trait.

Big Front

People with big front teeth can be very stubborn and have to be shown they are wrong before they change their minds. These folks tend to be impatient and need constant reassurance. They have the ability to hold their ground when faced with challenges.

Chapter 15
THE JAW

"My face is my livelihood." ~ *Kramer (Seinfeld, March 26, 1999)*

People's jaws show physical power, resolve, and intensity. The jaw reveals information about a person's principles, ethics, and how they handle conflict. This facial feature is related to physical stamina and personal tenacity.

Wide

People who have wide jaws have physical staying power and rarely admit defeat regardless of the odds. They tend to be really committed and faithful to their principles and have a strong need to control others. These folks will hang in there even in the most difficult situations.

Narrow

A person with narrow jaws tends to avoid any type of physical disagreement. They are less aggressive and combative than someone with wide jaws and will continually seek consensus. While they have no desire to control others, they resist someone trying to rule or dominate them.

Jowls

People with jowls command respect, because jowls are considered symbols of authority and personal power. Folks with this feature have a sense of great individual power and the ability to use it.

Chapter 16
The Chin

"God has given you one face and you make yourself another." ~ William Shakespeare

Chins indicate a person's ability to keep going when times get tough and to rebound from trauma or disappointment. Chins also tell us how well people can take disapproval and rejection.

Large

A person with a strong and well-defined chin tends to be forceful, competitive, and aggressive. These folks have great determination and possess a survivor's character. They won't run from any kind of battle.

Small

People with small, delicate chins are sensitive and can be easily offended by disapproval or rejection. Because these folks are already hard on themselves, they don't need outside criticism to guide them. They do need support and validation from others. They are not very aggressive and have no interest in competitive situations.

Sticks Out

People whose chins stick out will usually get the last word in any conversation or quarrel. They can be an awesome opponent who never says quit. These folks cannot be easily frightened or pushed around.

Receding

Those people who have a receding chin avoid any type of discord. They seldom challenge anyone directly. They seek consensus over assertive or aggressive behavior. These folks have strong ethics and expect everyone to follow the same rules they do. They would rather follow orders than give them.

Broad

Those folks with broad chins have great physical stamina and can bounce back from tribulation and continue on their way. They are able to garner support and help from others when responding to challenges. They are not as easily offended as someone with a small chin.

Very Broad

People with very broad chins are incredibly tough and are capable of bouncing back from a loss that would destroy most people. They are physically expressive and sex is an important form of communication for them. This is the chin found on most athletes.

Long

A person with a long chin has the same inborn power as the person with a broad chin. These folks are in touch with the physical world. They tend to be well-grounded, but they may need to think more before they reveal their thoughts to others.

Round

People with round chins are compassionate, sympathetic, and hospitable toward others. They are interested and very concerned about the well being of others. These folks tend to be considerate, and when something needs to be done, they always put people first.

Straight

A person with a straight chin is serious and motivated by what they believe in. They are idealistic and their focus is on getting the job done. These folks enjoy debating, especially when they feel strongly about something.

Pointed

People who are endowed with a pointed chin are focused on staying in control. They have a talent for getting their own way. Accomplishing their goals is what is important to them. These folks don't like having anyone tell them what to do without first giving them a complete explanation.

Very Pointed

A person with a very pointed chin, especially if it is long and protruding, tends to be very domineering in getting their own way. They can be insensitive in almost any situation and are uncompromising and resourceful in achieving their goals. Smart and oversensitive, they usually suffer from mood swings. With these folks, meeting their goals comes before people's feelings.

Chapter 17
Face Shapes

"I think your whole life shows in your face and you should be proud of that." ~
Lauren Bacall

Reading face shapes begins with an overview of the face, specifically the height and width of the head and face. People with a well-developed back of the head tend to be more emotional and family and communally orientated. The narrower the back of head is, the less evident this trait becomes. A high crown indicates a person's self-assurance; while a low crown suggests that a person may have less confidence. Conformity can be detected by the width or narrowness of the head when viewed from the front. Since the length of the head reveals forethought, a person with a short head, when viewed from the side, has a tendency toward less caution and more of a live-life-in-the-moment attitude.

For the face reader, the overall shape of the face can reveal a way to quickly and effectively increase the ability to form an instant and precise impression. For example, as discussed in Chapter 5, "The 60 Second Read," divide the face into three areas: the upper zone from the eyebrows to the hairline (the original hairline), the middle zone from the eyebrows to the bottom of the nose, and the bottom zone from the bottom of the nose to the bottom of the chin (the last chin if there is more than one).

People with an obviously large upper zone are focused on anything mental. They are interested in all the details and facts that are available.

A person with a predominant middle zone is someone who is ambitious, with a strong need for position and status. They prefer getting to the point and don't require or need all the details.

Someone who has a very large bottom zone is a down-to-earth and grounded person. They don't like to be pushed or crowded into a corner. These folks like to make up their own minds in their own time.

The way different features of the face relate to one another can tell great deal about a person's history. Looking at face shapes, categories, combinations, dominance, profiles, and head types will give the face reader the pieces needed to read an individual's complete life story and personality traits.

FACE SHAPE

There are several distinct face shapes that indicate key characteristics about its owner.

Broad

People with broad faces, wide or square, reveal a natural self-assurance and the appearance of great strength and power. These folks are used to getting what they want—respect for their views and ideas. They are comfortable in leadership positions.

Narrow

A person with a narrow face is not naturally self-confident; it's something they have to learn. These folks are full of pride about what they have learned and look for chances to apply what they know. They are more comfortable working independently than managing others.

Diamond

Someone who is endowed with a diamond-shaped face, widest at cheeks, has a very quick and decisive mind. They are impatient and when they want something they want it immediately. These folks abhor slowness in others. However, they don't want to be pushed or pressured when making decisions.

Trapezoid

Someone who has a face shaped like a trapezoid, broadest under the cheeks, likes to keep tranquility around them by hiding behind their own feelings. These folks should not be taken too lightly, because they can be very tenacious and strongly opinionated.

Flat

People with a flat face tend to be polite and tend to avoid the limelight. They are honest about their feelings and are unusually helpful and sharing. These folks get through life without much upheaval or unnecessary validation for what they do.

FACE CATEGORY

A person's face category is one more way of looking at facial features as a whole to disclose basic personality traits about the person. In classifying faces, there is a combination of facial distinctiveness that lets the face reader know more about the link between facial features and personality. According to physiognomist Mac Fulfer, J.D., there are three basic face categories and variations of each one.

Large Square Face – Physical

People who have a large, square face and big jaws and chin are considered physical types. They are doers and respond to life with action. They tend to be competitive and love physical activities. They need freedom and personal space, and when distressed, they want to do something about it immediately.

Narrow Face – Thinker

A person with a thin face, large forehead, and small jaw or chin is considered a mental type. Their focus is internal and intellectual, and these folks are more connected to their inner thoughts and feelings than to their outer world. When concerned, they like to solve their own challenges.

Round Face – Emotional

Someone who has a round face, round chin, and full cheeks is considered an emotional type. These folks connect with others easily and are very people oriented. They love parties, good food, and sharing with others. They relish group activities, especially planning and directing them.

Broad Face/Square Chin – Thinker/Physical

A person with a broad forehead and a square chin is considered a mental physical type. They like to do mental work in connection with some form of physical or mechanical activity. These folks are active doers and love to plan projects.

High Broad Forehead/ Round Chin – Thinker/Emotional

People with a high, broad forehead and a round chin are considered a mental/emotional type. They enjoy people and planning, but with a decided intellectual approach. They connect with people's feelings but are inclined to keep their own feelings to themselves. These folks are very capable directors and good managers.

Square Face/Round Chin – Physical/Emotional

Someone with a square face and a round chin is considered a physical/emotional type. They have a strong people orientation and excel at planning group activities. They enjoy being physically active in whatever is going on. They combine a strong physical drive with a good mechanical ability, a love of physical comfort, and a good sense of direction.

Facial Dominance

Large Upper Zone

A person with a large upper zone, from the eyebrows to the original hairline, focuses on thinking. They want to know how and why things are different from one another. They enjoy the world of ideas and acquire knowledge in areas where they have an interest.

Small Upper Zone

People who have a small upper zone, from the eyebrows to the original hairline, tend to be very strong-minded, determined, and passionate. Once they make up their minds about something, these folks are not easily deterred.

Large Middle Zone

Someone with a large middle zone, from the eyebrows to the bottom of the nose, focuses on position, opulence, and excellence. These folks are ambitious in carrying out their goals and dreams, but what they really want is to be envied by others for their successes.

Small Middle Zone

A person with a small middle zone, from the eyebrows to the bottom of the nose, tends to be someone who gives more than one hundred percent to everything they do, especially at work. These folks are well respected and the go-to person in many organizations.

Large Lower Zone

People who have a large lower zone, from the bottom of the nose to the bottom of the last chin, are grounded and sensible. They are apt to be physically tough and earthy. These folks have a good sense of themselves and their surroundings. They tend to project integrity and genuineness.

Small Lower Zone

Someone with a small lower zone, from the bottom of the nose to the bottom of the last chin, is very sensitive and doesn't do well with criticism. They are much more connected to their inner world than their outer world. These folks are not very physical and shy away from any kind of physical work.

Profile Category

Profile categories are a combination of facial features that form a method of pointing out a specific personality trait or traits. For example, a convex profile includes a sloping forehead, large nose with a high bridge, eyes that are full, and a mouth that juts further out than the chin. Conversely, a concave profile has a full round forehead that sticks out at the hairline, deep-set eyes, a shallow nose bridge, a concave nose, and a chin that extends beyond the lips. Profile combinations that are both convex and concave will have the characteristics of both. The upper face is about thinking and the lower face is about implementing those thoughts.

Convex

A person with a convex profile, where the forehead angles back and nose sticks out, has a quick mind that is at its best with systems and procedures. These folks are practical thinkers who can be impulsive and impatient at times. They are very comfortable managing others.

Moderately Convex

Someone with a moderately convex profile has the same attributes as the convex and very convex profiles, but to a lesser degree. These folks are more successful in getting more cooperation from others, because they tend to have more self-control.

Very Convex

People that have a very convex profile, where the nose is prominent and at sharp angles to the forehead and chin, have the ability to see something done once and then do it themselves. They are very observant and have a lot of energy. These folks are confident and quick to act, sometimes a little too aggressively.

Concave

People with a concave profile, where the forehead and chin stick out further than the center of the face, are creative problem solvers. They are inclined to be patiently determined, but when confronted they can be immovable. These folks also have a tendency to be too cautious and are definitely not risk takers.

Very Concave

People with an extremely concave profile, where the forehead and chin project more than nose, are good-natured idealists who usually don't display an aggressive nature. These folks may have a tendency to drag their feet when forced to make a decision.

Balanced

Someone with a balanced profile, neither convex nor concave, tends to have a good sense of balance between their outer life and their inner life. They also have the innate ability to think quickly or to think deeply. These folks are versatile and can apply themselves in many directions.

Convex-Concave

People with convex-concave profiles, where the forehead slants back and the chin sticks out, tend to have great memories. They are quick, practical thinkers who are patient in action and very tactful when they speak. Choosing their language carefully, these folks can say much with few words.

Concave-Convex

Those people who have concave-convex profiles, where the forehead is full and the chin recedes, use an emotional approach to their work and seek recognition for their hard work. These folks have a propensity to act before thinking about the consequences of their actions.

Head Category

The shape of a person's head gives clear clues to their personality. There are four basic head types that are distinctive enough to be read at a glance: low forehead/high crown, high forehead/low crown, round and square.

Low Forehead/High Crown

People with a low forehead and high crown can be very disbelieving and demand facts as the basis for making their decisions. They can be determined, controlling, unrelenting, and very hard to persuade. These folks are comfortable with power and are constantly searching for it.

High Forehead/Low Crown

The person with a high forehead and low crown is a positive individual who wants to believe in others. They have a propensity to be trusting, compassionate, and considerate. These folks also have a tendency to become discouraged in the face of adversity and misfortune

Round

Someone with a round head, where the widest part is just above the ears, is a fearless controlling force who tends to charge ahead in a sometimes thoughtless and impetuous fashion.

Square

People with square heads, where head rises above the ears to a flat top, are very guarded in their approach to life. These folks are dependable and less passionate than someone without this feature. They also have a tendency to not fight for their viewpoints straightforwardly, preferring an indirect approach.

Chapter 18
Lines and Marks

"Wrinkles are God's Makeup" ~ *Rose Rosetree*

Reading and understanding facial marks is a very important aspect of face reading. Facial marks include lines, dimples, clefts, moles, blemishes, birthmarks, and facial hair.

When reading facial marks, remember that the more defined and pronounced the mark the stronger the personality trait. Also keep in mind that the right side of the face represents a person's public or business side and the left side of the face represents a person's personal or internal world.

LINES

FOREHEAD

Multiple Horizontal Lines

People with multiple horizontal lines in their foreheads have many different interests in life and have developed strong mental and emotional ties regarding those abilities. Lines that go all the way across the forehead indicate a high level of intellectual development toward specific interests.

Single Horizontal Line

A person with a single horizontal line on their forehead has a strong passion for something or someone. These folks are driven internally and can easily become obsessed with that person or object.

Vertical or Diagonal Lines

People who have vertical or diagonal lines on their forehead have experienced a lot of mental strain in developing a way to deal with or understand a particular challenge. In other words, these folks have given intense attention to a challenge that required a great deal of concentration and self-discipline.

Single Vertical Line

Someone who has a single vertical line in the middle of the forehead has what is called a freight train or determination line. These folks will let nothing stand in their way once they've made up their minds and are focused on a goal. This line has also been referred to as a mark of devotion, which means the person with this feature struggles to live in harmony with his or her highest principles.

LINES BETWEEN THE EYEBROWS

Two Short Vertical Lines

People who have two short vertical lines between the eyebrows are very hard on themselves. These self-critics set high standards for themselves and expect others to meet those same standards. This feature can reveal a self-destructive nature or can simply mean this person is doing everything possible to make sure they're right and not caught off guard. These folks rarely settle for second best.

Three or More Vertical Lines

A person with three short vertical lines between the eyebrows is inclined to be a perfectionist. These folks set impossibly high and rigid achievement standards, are motivated more by fear of failure than by the fear of success, and measure their own worth entirely by their productivity and accomplishments.

Triangle Lines

People who have lines that form a triangle between the eyebrows have exceptional visionary insight. These folks have a strong connection between the left and right sides of their brain allowing them to have access to their inner vision and knowledge. They are able to use logic and feelings in a balanced way to make the right decisions.

Several Fine Horizontal Lines

A person with several fine horizontal lines across the bridge of their nose has the tendency to take on too much responsibility. If the responsibility becomes too heavy, a single horizontal line will form (see below).

Single Horizontal Line

Someone with a single horizontal line on the bridge of their nose is overly responsible. The result is burnout. They tend to force themselves to keep doing something that is no longer emotionally or mentally satisfying. When an individual reaches this point, they need to find something else to alleviate the load they feel they are carrying.

LinesRadiating From Eyes

People with lines that radiate out of the outside corners of their eyes, sometimes called crow's feet, always see the big picture. These folks are hard to fool, because they have a greater understanding of issues and how they are related. In other words, they are not gullible.

Diagonal Lines on Cheeks

A person with diagonal lines below the eyes on the cheeks has what are considered resolve or bravery lines. These lines represent the conquering of difficult circumstances. This person had to reach deep into their psyche to find the key to dealing with a very difficult time in their life.

Nose Wrinkles

People with wrinkles on each side of their nose when they are smiling or laughing tend to have a good sense of humor. They may be playful and sometimes a little mischievous. They enjoy making the people around them feel comfortable.

Nose to Mouth Lines

Someone who has lines that drop down from the nose to near the corner of the mouth has what are referred to as disappointment lines. These folks have experienced discontent and disillusionment in their lives. The more intense the line is, the deeper the disappointment. It is not uncommon to observe a line on just one side of the face, or deeper on one side than the other.

Mouth to Chin Lines

People with lines from the corner of the mouth to the chin have what are called empathy or sorrow lines. These lines are normally associated with grief or great emotional pain. These folks tend to have great compassion and sympathy for others who may be suffering.

Dimple Lines

A person with encouragement lines, dimples that are shaped like lines, has the ability to help people feel better about themselves. In turn people tend to look up to and respect the person with this facial trait.

Vertical Lines on Upper Lip

Someone who has a series of vertical lines just above the upper lip means this person is a survivor. Tried and tested, these folks can handle just about anything that comes their way, because they have already experienced adversity that might be as bad as it gets.

Chin to Cheeks Lines

People who have a continuous line that runs under the chin and up the cheeks, sometimes called a gab line, have a natural gift for talking. They seldom run out of things to say and never meet a stranger. This line shows most prominently when the person smiles, which is something they do easily.

Chin Arch

Some people have an arched line on their chin just below the mouth, which is an indication of their need to be desirable. For these folks there could be a low self-esteem issue involved, causing them to validate their self-worth through outside sources.

Mouth Crescents

A person with indents or crescents at the corner of their mouth has a secret. There are some areas of their lives that are taboo or too painful to share with anyone. If these folks do open up and tell someone their hidden truths, the lines will disappear.

Chin Bumps

Someone with a chin that has a tense, bumpy appearance tends to be a cynic who is always prepared for the worst. These folks will face almost any challenge, and tend to be tough and hardened in order to protect their rather pessimistic attitude.

131

Ear Crease

People who have a vertical line on their ear lobe are susceptible to medical problems related to the heart. They are generally very hard on themselves and tend to be stressed out and anxious.

DIMPLES AND CLEFTS

The difference between dimples and clefts is that the dimple can be found in the cheek or chin and a cleft can be found in the chin or the nose. The dimple in the chin has more of a rounded shape, as opposed to a cleft, which is shaped more like a valley or crevasse.

Cheek Dimples

A person with a dimple in their cheek or cheeks is all about playfulness related to a romantic nature. To love or be loved with all of the emotional commitment that goes with it is very important to the folks with this facial trait.

Chin Dimple

Someone with a dimple in their chin indicates that they are a good sport. These folks are very good-natured and usually have a very playful personality. Their playfulness is related to more of a fun-loving than serious nature.

Chin Cleft

People who have a cleft in their chin are very adventurous and playful. They like to maintain control of their lives and relationships. They are also very adaptable and may go through many jobs and relationships if the ones they are in do not satisfy them.

Nose Cleft

A person with a small cleft or line in the end of their nose is someone who is still searching for their niche in life. They may have trouble with money. They have a tendency to set up tight budgets but cannot resist the urge to spend when it comes to something they can't resist. These folks may also exhibit nitpicky behavior because they are frantically searching for that something that will satisfy their emotional and psychological needs.

MOLES, BIRTHMARKS AND BLEMISHES

These facial marks can be large or small, flat or raised, smooth or warty, or with hair growing from them. These skin-level marks reveal some interesting facts about a person's character and personality traits.

MOLES AND BIRTHMARKS

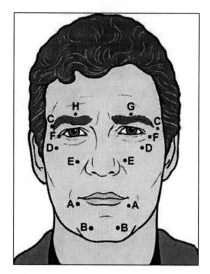

A. Indicates a decisive nature

B. Indicates an aggressive trait

C. Indicates a thoughtful trait

D. Indicates a natural beauty spot, also a lack of authority

E. Indicates an attraction toward intellectual matters

F. Indicates an honest, straightforward trait

G. Indicates a tendency toward laziness

H. Indicates determination and assertiveness

BLEMISHES

The challenges of life and their corresponding emotions and vulnerability will become visible in the face in the form of blemishes. For example, pimples are all about anger; boils and cysts are about seething anger; warts are a result of shame; freckles are more about determination and rebellion; age spots reveal a culmination of difficult learning.

Chapter 19

APPLICATIONS

"Nature gives you the face you have at twenty; it is up to you to merit the face you have at fifty." ~ *Coco Chanel*

Face reading has as many applications as there are faces. The information contained in this book is written with an emphasis on business and personal applications. However, these skills and techniques are also useful for jury selection, law enforcement specialists, teachers, and medical professionals, just to name a few.

There are other methods of understanding a person's personality besides face reading. For example, personality type tests, NLP, handwriting analysis, astrology, numerology, and even chiromancy (palm reading) all point out some kind of personality profile. Face reading is different from all other methods in one very important way: The results do not depend on outside information from the person who is being analyzed. In face reading, the person being studied does not have to take a test; respond honestly; produce a handwriting sample; provide a name, birth date, place of birth; or hold out their hand. If they have a face, it can be read with great accuracy.

Making a rapid and precise character read of someone's face does not depend on their mental or physical ability, truthfulness, or collaboration, and is without a doubt a most effective and useful tool. It is relevant to a person's personal and public worlds, including leading, selling, managing, marketing, negotiations, hiring the right person for the right job, teaching, training, relationships, jury selection, law enforcement, medical professionals, and the list goes on and on. In effect, face reading offers an advantage in anything that has to do with open interaction, persuasion, or communication between people.

Another benefit of face reading over the other methods of personality typing is that it happens almost instantly. Other approaches require that some technique must be learned before it can be of use. Physiognomy, on the other hand, can be deliberate with each and every person a face reader meets. By becoming skilled at reading one feature at a time, the face reader builds upon his or her skills until they can see every face as a gateway to a person's personal and public personality.

FACE READING TIPS

When reading a face in detail—a process that requires at least an hour—face readers will find layer upon layer of information, including some contradictions. It is in this process that personality traits begin to emerge.

When beginning to read facial features, always look for all the traits that are associated with a particular feature. There may be more than one contributing trait to the overall effect of that specific feature. For example, when reading someone's eyes, look for their size, color, and width and note if they are recessed or bulging, and slanted up or down. The combination of these characteristics contributes to the connection between the feature and the person's personality. Use this system as you read each feature of a person's face.

Remember to look for the verys, or extremes, of a particular feature when analyzing a face. The deeper or larger the feature, the greater its effectiveness. For example, the more someone's ears protrude, the less conforming they are. If the right ear sticks out more than the left ear, it indicates a more non-conforming and independent public persona.

It is important to keep in mind that certain features combined with other features can increase or diminish that particular feature's effectiveness. For example, coarse hair and fine-textured skin or fine hair and coarse-textured skin indicate that the person with these features has a personality that is somewhere between being reserved and being open.

The traits associated with a person's facial features are a roadmap to their personality in every area and situation of their life. For example, a person with straight eyebrows makes most of their decisions based on logic and needs all the facts before proceeding. Folks with curved eyebrows connect best through their understanding of people, and they are not particularly interested in having all the details before they make a decision.

Each personality trait connected to a particular facial feature applies to not just the person you are reading, but to everyone who has that trait. For example, someone with a flat forehead is a sequential thinker. Someone with bulging eyes loves to contribute and talk, and if they also have a slanted forehead, coarse hair and skin, the talking trait is even more empathized.

Here are a few more things to keep in mind as you begin to read faces.

1. Don't read a face too quickly, and keep everything in context.

2. Look for extremes, or verys. (On a scale of 1-10 with 10 the most extreme)

3. If a feature is not an extreme or very (1-4 on a scale of 1-10), don't read it.

4. Read each face as being unique. Don't compare it to others.

5. Don't get caught up in typecasting gender or race.

6. Read lines and blemishes in perspective.

7. Read someone's face as carefully as you would read your own.

The following sample face-reading applications give the face reader a quick reference guide to each feature and its corresponding personality trait. This is a good starting place for using face reading in other applications. Once the face reader understands what to look for in a particular reading, it's easy to apply the skill to other areas.

Face Reading and Persuasion

Group Persuasion

When making a presentation or selling to a committee or group, pay close attention to each member's face to determine who to address your comments to at the appropriate time.

Broad Face

Begin by determining which person has the most personal power. People with broad faces, wide or square, reveal a natural self-confidence and the appearance of great strength and power. This is the person you need to convince, because others will tend to follow his or her lead. These folks go ahead with decisions, regardless of the approval or disapproval of others.

Large Nose

When discussing money, give your attention to the person who has the largest nose. People who have a very large nose tip have a strong interest in gaining financial security, especially an adequate cash flow. They speak with authority on money matters and may also be a collector. They are accustomed to having a great deal of impact on others. Let them know the costs and benefits of your proposal.

Jowls

If a member of the committee is endowed with a large jaw or jowls, remember these folks are used to getting their way. People with jowls command respect, because jowls are symbols of authority and personal power. They designate a person's sense of personal power and an ability to use it. Be respectful, listen, and expect to be questioned.

Largest Chin

Look for the person with the largest chin when you're ready for someone to get in the last word. People whose chins stick out will usually get the last word in any discussion or argument. They are a formidable adversary who never says quit. They cannot be easily intimidated or bluffed. When situations turn competitive, these folks expect to win, and usually do.

INDIVIDUAL PERSUASION

FACIAL COLORING

Light-Colored

Light-colored people tend to live in a more unstructured manner. They are more open-minded, less focused, and are attracted to variety. They respond favorably to new ideas, colors, places, styles, improvements, and features. When it comes to business, they are all business. When communicating with a light-colored person, communicate quickly, enthusiastically, respectfully, and always give them a choice.

Dark-Colored

Dark-colored people carry on in a more conservative manner. They are not as spontaneous as the light-colored person. They tend to be serious minded, more focused, and they don't thrive on variety. They bore easily, handle details well, and are not apt to change their minds. When it comes to business, dark-colored people like to talk about their family and friends. They're not all about business. When communicating with a dark-colored person, communicate slowly, thoroughly, and convincingly.

FACIAL DOMINANCE

Large Zone 1

The person with a large Zone 1 focuses on thinking. These people are fascinated with the world of ideas and want to acquire knowledge, especially in areas of personal interest. Give them complete explanations with all the details. These folks think everything through and make decisions based on doing so. Feelings and emotions don't play much of a role in their thinking processes.

Large Zone 2

People with a large Zone 2 tend to focus on money, status, luxury, and quality. They may also be ambitious, going into action to reach their goals and dreams, but their secret desire is to be envied by everyone for their success. These are people who are driven by their feelings and emotions. They make decisions based on something feeling right. These folks enjoy the status of owning the best material things.

Large Zone 3

The person with a large Zone 3 is down to earth and views life in a physical way. They have a good sense of themselves and their physical surroundings. When they say something will work, they've already checked to make sure it will. When they have a problem or need to make a decision, they do their best thinking when they can do something physical. These folks love antidotes and stories, but let them make up their own minds.

EYEBROWS

Straight

Those people with straight eyebrows are direct and want the facts and all the details. They make decisions based on logic and need to be shown all the facts before accepting something as true. They generally don't let emotions affect their way of thinking. They are consistent and well balanced in their emotions and behavior. Their approach is logical, direct, and factual. The emphasis is on details and ideas.

Curved

Folks who are endowed with curved eyebrows are people oriented. They connect to the world best through their understanding of people. They prefer not to be burdened with too many details without seeing a real-world application. They are generally very receptive to all types of people. They are good listeners and are open to other's opinions and ideas. The emphasis is on how a product or service helps people feel better.

Arched

For the person with arched or angled eyebrows there is the need to stay mentally in control of any situation in which they find themselves. Always ask for their opinion and let them feel they are in control. These folks are imaginative, clever with words, and hate to be wrong. The emphasis is to give them a chance to shape the conversation.

Tangled

People with tangled eyebrows often find themselves in conflict with others. They love to challenge other people's knowledge about a certain subject just for the sake of seeing if there are any hidden facts. These folks are unconventional thinkers who have many and varied interests. When this person challenges you, and they will, don't get rattled; just explain your proposition clearly and succinctly.

Executive

A person with this set of unique eyebrows—thinner in Area 1 and thicker in Area 3—is usually very well organized. These folks are noted for their thoroughness and can be counted upon to cover all the fine points. Obviously, give them all the details and technicalities. Don't try to bluff this person, just know what you are talking about and stick to it.

FACE SHAPE

Broad

People with broad, wide, or square faces reveal a natural self-confidence and the appearance of strength and power. These folks are used to getting what they want, including respect for their views and ideas. Let them express themselves and give them a complete presentation.

Narrow

A person with a thin face is not naturally self-assured. They have had to learn to be confident. They are full of pride about what they have learned and look for opportunities to apply what they know. These folks don't usually put themselves out until they are very sure about what they know. Ask them for their opinion and respect their research and knowledge.

Diamond

Someone who is endowed with a diamond-shaped face, widest at cheeks, has a very quick and decisive mind. They are impatient, and when they want something, they want it immediately. These folks abhor slowness in others. However, they don't want to be pushed when making decisions. Get to the point with these folks as quickly as possible.

Trapezoid

Someone who has a face shaped like a trapezoid (broadest below the cheeks) likes to keep the peace by hiding their own emotions. They should not be underestimated, because they are very tenacious and strongly opinionated. Always ask for their input over and over or they will put up road blocks to your proposition. The emphasis is these folks hate to argue, so make it safe for them to complain.

Flat

People with a flat face tend to be polite and are inclined to avoid the limelight. They are honest about their feelings and are unusually helpful and sharing. These folks get through life without much upheaval or unnecessary validation for what they do. Give these individuals a complete presentation without a lot of bells and whistles.

Eyes

The eyes are the features people look at first when meeting someone. Eyes can also tell when people filter or screen out information.

Large

People with large, full irises connect with their feelings and are more likely to show and express what they are feeling. They also have a visual, hands-on approach and need to see the information they receive. They listen best when they are looking at the person talking or what that person is talking about. These folks tend to be honest and trustworthy, expecting the same from others.

Small

People with small irises tend to show little emotion and can be affected by people's actions and arguments. These folks are motivated by physical expressions of encouragement and acceptance. They guard against someone trying to deceive or manipulate them. They like to make decisions with their head rather than with their emotions. Stick to the facts with these individuals.

Angle Upward

If the eyes angle up, the person is an optimist, inspirational, and has a good imagination. These folks focus on the positive things in life. They expect things to turn out for the best. Mirror their optimistic attitude.

Angle Downward

People with eyes that angle down expect problems and are especially good at spotting potential difficulties. Don't be too demonstrative or too enthusiastic with these folks who are almost always very serious. The emphasis is to work together to solve challenges one by one.

Bulging

People with eyes that seem to bulge out are naturally enthusiastic and eager to participate. They don't have to run the show, but they want to be included in everything that is happening. These folks love to talk and if interrupted tend to feel hurt and may put up emotional barriers, feeling they are not appreciated. The emphasis is to listen to them and include them in all facets of the presentation.

Recessed

Those people who have recessed eyes appear to be calm and relaxed, but are, in fact, intense, resolute, and continually evaluating everything around them. They question things carefully and need proof before accepting anything. Don't push these folks, and above all let them make up their own minds.

Straight Lower Eyelid

Those folks who have straight bottom lids try to maintain an emotional distance or self-protective stance. They keep their guard up and can be tough to approach. Once you gain their trust, however, they can be a most loyal friend and supporter. The emphasis is on answering all their questions openly and honestly.

NOSE

Long and Straight

People with long and straight noses are logical, long-range planers and strategists. Don't try emotional tactics with these folks. It's all about logic and facts. The emphasis is on using a logical and systematic presentation.

Concave

Folks with concave noses allow feelings and emotions to have an important impact on their decision making. These folks respond very well to emotional tactics. They must receive some kind of positive acknowledgement for their efforts. The emphasis is on appealing to their feelings.

Convex

People with convex or aquiline noses appreciate beauty and elegance, but their real talent is in creative problem solving. They can usually see better ways to do things and are not afraid to try them. Listen to their opinions and be aware of their concern for cost versus value. The emphasis is on putting some beauty into the proposition.

MOUTH

Up Turned

A person with an upturned mouth listens with an optimistic attitude. They always hear only the best in what others tell them. Mirror their demeanor and ask for their opinions.

Down Turned

Those people with mouths that turn down tend to mistrust what others tell them. They generally don't have high expectations so are not disappointed when things don't turn out the way they hoped. When selling to these folks, always underpromise and over-deliver.

Full Lower Lip

The person with a full lower lip has the ability to convince others of their point of view, especially about the external world of facts and figures. They have a natural gift of persuasion. Selling to this person means you must know your product or service as well as your competitor's, because these folks will have done their research before they decide to buy.

Full Upper Lip

People with a full upper lip are outspoken and straight forward. These folks have a strong radar system that quickly detects deception in others. To sell this person, make sure everything you tell them is the absolute truth. A gross exaggeration or lie will cause them not to buy. The emphasis is to honor their passion for truthfulness.

Thin Lips

Those people with very thin lips tend to be reserved, cautious, and don't trust easily. They especially mistrust flattery and verbal expressions of emotion. These folks are very careful not to express anything that would expose them to criticism. Make these individuals feel right and use open-ended questions. The emphasis is not to talk about anything personal.

TEETH

Even Teeth

People with even teeth have a logical approach and learn life's lessons quickly. They make decisions with poise and self-confidence. They have strong inner balance and get along well with others. If this person has straight eyebrows, make your presentation based on facts and logic.

Gap

A person with a gap between their front teeth is willing to take risks even when they're not sure of the results. They make intuitive decisions in the moment. The larger the gap between the teeth, the stronger the trait. When selling to this person, remember they tend to make decisions based on intuition and calculated risks.

Big Front Teeth

People with big front teeth can be very stubborn and have to be shown they are wrong before they change their minds. They have the ability to hold their ground when faced with opposition. If this person feels they have been put in an untenable position by the salesperson, no sale will take place.

Crooked Teeth

Those people who have crooked teeth, especially the bottom teeth, tend to see both sides of every issue. Holding themselves to extremely high standards, they hate to be wrong so they often double check their facts before doing anything. Help this buyer see the best possible scenario for making the decision to buy.

EARS

High

People with high tops (even or higher than the eye level) tend to absorb information immediately. These folks approach life with a "let's do it now" mentality. They are more interested in seeing results. Doing it right is not as important as getting it done now. Sometimes this causes them to overlook important details. The emphasis is to give them just enough information to make up their mind.

Low

The folks with low bottoms (lower than bottom of the nose) have a "let's do it right" line of attack. Patient listeners, they may feel they will miss something if they are forced to rush. They are always ready to hear more. These folks make buying decisions in a thoughtful, deliberate way. The emphasis is don't close too early.

Chapter 20
SAMPLE READINGS

"It's hard to see your own face without a mirror." ~ Phillip C. McGraw

Now that you've seen examples of how facial features are read and how each face reflects both genetics and life experiences, it's time to look at some sample readings. With practice you'll start to see the jumble of puzzle pieces that is the human face start to come together. Remember, physiognomy is not a substitute for good old common sense. Don't get so engrossed in reading a face that you ignore the obvious. Watch what a person does; compare it to what they are saying; then read their face.

According to physiognomist Rose Rosetree, a face reader must be very careful when reading facial verys, or extremes. By now you are probably aware of all the verys on your own face. Remember, it is not uncommon to have a dislike for someone who behaves in a way that is completely opposite of your own "very" feature. In other words, when you have extreme traits in one direction and the person you are trying to read has extreme traits in the opposite direction, you can easily misread their face.

Unfortunately, this aversion operates unconsciously. The way around this dilemma is to catch the feeling of dislike when you first feel it and just become neutral about that person's verys and interpret what they really mean. Once you are conscious of this possible prejudice, it's easier to do an accurate and complete reading.

As you begin to read faces and see how features relate to one another, you begin to see the complete story of the person's life. You now have a communication tool that is responding in the moment to the person's every thought and feeling.

In the following face samples you will begin to actually read faces. The best way to start reading is to look at the illustrated example and read what you can see before you read the explanation. Identify all the features and lines that you can see and then look up their meaning.

Use the feature checklist on page 190 to help you systematically read any face accurately.

SAMPLE READING
NORMA JEANE

Feature

Facial Coloring

   Light Colored

Hair and Skin

Description

She lived a fairly
unstructured life. She
was usually more open-
mined and very attracted
to variety.

Combination

She had mood swings. One moment she enjoyed things on a grand scale, and the next moment she was looking for a quiet place to hide. She enjoyed being the center of attention at social gatherings, becoming very approachable and sometimes bold and forceful. At times she could be very idealistic and critical.

Forehead

Flat

She was a sequential thinker, who liked things in a step-by-step order. If too much information was presented too fast or out of sequence, she would just shut down. However, once she learned something she retained it for life.

Wide

She had a very large ego and protected herself from showing any signs of weakness. She was at times an idealist who had a lot of ideas to contribute. She was courageous and handled unfamiliar situations without fear.

Eyebrows

Arched/Angled

She had to stay mentally in control of any situation in which she was involved. At times she could be outgoing and open, and had the ability to be detached. She was clever with words and disliked being wrong. She had a global view of whatever interested her.

Middlebrow

She was flexible and was not apt to blurt out information, and at the same time she wasn't as guarded as a highbrow.

Starters	She had starter eyebrows which meant she had a talent for new projects and ideas but lost interest in them about halfway through.

Eyes

Wide	She tended to be broadminded with a far-sighted imagination. She always saw the big picture, which means she sometimes missed some important details. She was very tolerant when reacting to situations and would put up with a lot before she reacted.
Large	She connected with her feelings and expressed them freely. She had a visual, hands-on approach to life. She listened best when there was constant eye contact. She was honest and trustworthy and expected the same from others.

Angle – Level	She really had a balanced view of life and tended to be pragmatic and objective. She was not easily discouraged and was resilient under stress.
Depth – Recessed	She appeared to be calm but in fact was intense, possessive, and continually evaluating her world. While she accepted things as they appeared, she usually needed proof before accepting things as fact. She protected her inner self by being thoughtful and cautious.
Color	Her blue eyes indicate she had a tendency to tell someone exactly what was on her mind. She was at times spontaneous and willful, and was a highly sensual and sensitive person. She also enjoyed flirting.

Eyelids

Upper not Visible	She had the ability to focus and required her own personal space. She disliked demands placed on her by others when she was focused. She was capable of intimacy, but only when she was ready for it.
Lower Straight	She maintained an emotional distance and was self-protective. At times she was guarded and difficult to approach. But once she accepted someone she became a most loyal supporter and friend.

Eyelashes

Long	She was tolerant and accepting and sometimes had a gentle disposition.

Eye Padding

Harry Perdew, Ph.D.

| Moderate | She sometimes focused on her external environment to the extent of ignoring her own needs, resulting in her becoming impatient, overly sensitive, critical, and even disagreeable. |

Nose

| Shape – Concave | She allowed her feelings and emotions to have an important impact on her work. She did very well in a supportive environment but struggled in a non-supportive one. She could accomplish almost anything if she received some appreciation for her work. |
| Tip – Large Ball | She was very concerned with scarcity and interested in gaining financial or emotional security. She was also enjoyed collecting things. |

Nostrils – Round	She was usually willing to give, sometimes to a fault, of her time and money. She easily shared what she had with those close to her.

Ears

Close to Head	She preferred to conform to known social values and follow instructions. She enjoyed belonging to groups, albeit sometimes from a distance. She did not want to appear too different from other people. She generally preferred to do what was expected of her and follow procedures.
Lobes – Large	She had a fascination with physical reality and had a good memory that helped her anticipate major problems before they arose.

Cheeks

High

She was a head turner who immediately received attention when she entered a room. She was perceived to have leadership qualities, even though she did not think she did.

Wide

She had a lot of energy and endurance, which allowed her to go the distance. She approached challenges with a "can-do" attitude. She sometimes exhibited a slow but steady approach to things.

Mouth

Large

She tended to be demonstrative, outgoing, and sometimes talkative, showing a lot of confidence in expressing herself.

Up Turned	She was an optimist when listening to others. She tended to hear only the best in what others told her.
Lip – Full Lower	She had the ability to convince others of her point of view and enjoyed a natural gift of persuasion.

Chin

Broad	She had great physical endurance and was able to bounce back from setbacks easily. Her feelings were not hurt as easily as someone with a narrower chin.
Round	She showed compassion, sympathy, generosity, and hospitality toward others. She, for the most part, was kind-hearted and had the tendency to put others first.

Face

Shape – Broad	She had a natural self-confidence and gave the appearance of having great strength and power.
High Broad Forehead/ Round Chin	She enjoyed people and planning, but with an intellectual approach. She connected with other people's feelings but kept most of her feelings to herself.

Facial Dominance

Large Upper Zone	She was interested in how one thing is different from another. She really enjoyed the world of ideas and was always looking for information about the things that interested her.

Head Category

High Forehead/ Low Crown	She was a person with an optimistic view of the world—most of the time. She tended to be trusting, sympathetic, and caring. She sometimes became a bit discouraged in the face of adversity.

Lines

Disappointment	She had many disappointments in her personal and public worlds. Although she dealt with each disappointment, nevertheless she was haunted by a life of disenchantment.
Secrets	There were some deep secrets in her life that she would never allow to come out into the open.

Harry Perdew, Ph.D.

SAMPLE READING
THOMAS JEFFERSON

Feature

Facial Coloring

   Light Colored

Hair and Skin

Description

He lived a fairly unstructured life. He was usually more open-mined and very attracted to variety.

Fine Hair and Skin

He was a bit hypersensitive and his feelings were easily hurt. He preferred quality rather than quantity in his life. He had a lot of pride and set high standards for himself and those around him. Being an idealist, he was more interested in how people conducted themselves rather than how they looked.

Forehead

Round

He used imagination and originality in solving problems. He had a quick mind and responded very quickly to situations. Many of his decisions were based on past experiences. Mostly, he tended to deal more with the reaction to a problem than the problem itself. He was blessed with a great memory.

Wide

He had a very large ego and protected himself from showing any signs of weakness. He was, at least most of the time, an idealist who had a lot of ideas to contribute. He was fairly courageous and handled most situations without fear.

Brow Ridge

He was a rules type of person. Once he understood the rules and procedures, he followed them to the letter. He expected everyone around him to adhere to the same rules. He really did not like change and was a bit conservative.

Eyebrows

Straight

He always wanted the facts and all the details about anything that interested him. His decisions were more based on logic than on emotions. His usual approach to challenges was logical and direct. He had an expanded visual appreciation for his surroundings.

Middlebrow	He was flexible and was not apt to blurt out information, and at the same time he wasn't as guarded as a highbrow.
Eveners	He had a habit of starting projects and completing them. His thought processes were even and consistent, especially when it came to the details. He could be less than tolerant with anyone who was not detail oriented.
Thick	He was mentally active and had great intellectual power. He was able to take an idea to a new level. His ability to work on a variety of tasks at the same time was legendary. He was a composite multi-tasker.

Eyes

Large

He connected with his feelings and expressed them freely. He had a visual, hands-on approach to life. He listened best when there was constant eye contact. He was unabashedly honest and trustworthy and expected the same from others.

Angle – Level

He really had a balanced view of life and tended to be pragmatic and objective. He was not easily discouraged and was resilient under stress.

Depth - Recessed

He appeared to be calm but in fact was intense, possessive, and was continually evaluating his world. While he accepted things as they appeared, he usually needed proof before accepting things as fact. He protected his inner self by being thoughtful and cautious.

Color - Blue

His blue eyes indicate he had a tendency to tell someone exactly what was on his mind. He was at times spontaneous and willful and was a highly sensual and sensitive person. He also enjoyed being a bit of a flirt.

Eyelids

Upper – Heavy

His very visible upper eyelids showed his strong need for intimacy. He bonded with those close to him and was in the habit of sharing all aspects of his life with them. Ironically, although he was a detail-oriented person, sometimes he would finish other people's sentences if they weren't speaking fast enough. He wanted them to get to the point quickly.

Lower Straight

While his right lower eyelid had a natural curve, his left lower eyelid was straight, indicating that in his personal world he maintained an emotional distance and was self-protective. At times he was guarded and difficult to approach. But once he accepted someone he became a most loyal supporter and friend.

Eyelashes

Short

His short eyelashes were an indication of a sensitive nature and someone whose feelings could be easily hurt. He also had a tendency to be quick to anger.

Nose

Size – Large	He had an incredible need to make a major contribution to the work he did. He did his best work when he could be in a leadership position, because of his need to make a significant impact on his work. It was terribly important for him to know that what he did really made a difference.
Shape – Long and Convex	He had a gift for planning and strategy, which he used in all aspects of his life. He always wanted to be in charge of his work environment, where he could control the pace and priority of the work. His aquiline nose also indicates his ability to be a creative problem solver. He preferred to direct others so that everything would be accomplished efficiently.

Ridge – High	He preferred to work independently and needed to have control of his workspace to do his best. He disliked anyone looking over his shoulder while he worked.
Tip – Level	He was very dependable and had a pretty good business sense. He trusted others but was not easily fooled. He expressed a normal amount of patience when dealing with others.
Tip – Small Ball	He had a true appreciation for the arts and a need to be surrounded by beauty. He had an excellent eye for quality in all things. He had a very aesthetic and imaginative approach to life.
Nostrils – Flared	He was self-confident and sometimes extravagant. He had an intense energy that at times caused him to go to extremes. He had a habit of taking on many projects at once because he felt he was invincible.

Septum	He had a long septum, which indicated he was analytical by nature. He especially liked to analyze other people.

Ears

Stick Out	He was an independent, non-conforming theorist. He was an original, out-of-the-box thinker. He was a person with his own set of rules who tended to charge ahead.
Lobes – Large	He had a fascination with physical reality and a good memory that helped him anticipate major problems before they arose.
Height – Low	He had a "do it right" approach to whatever he did. He was a patient listener who didn't like to be rushed, thinking he might miss something if it was too hurried. He was always ready to hear more from others.

Cheeks

High

He was a head turner who immediately received attention when he entered a room. He was perceived to have leadership qualities, even though he did not think leadership was one of his strong points.

Mouth

Straight

He was an objective listener who was capable of reflecting back to others what they had said in a realistic manner.

Lips – Full

He was emotionally expressive and physically demonstrative. He had a good sense of humor and enjoyed expressing himself whenever the opportunity presented itself.

Jaw

Wide

He had a lot of physical stamina and seldom surrendered, regardless of the odds. He was truly committed and loyal to his ideals and principles, with a tendency to dominate others.

Chin

Sticks Out

He usually got the last word in any discussion or debate. He was a formidable adversary that never quit. He was not easily intimidated or bluffed.

Broad

He had great physical endurance and was able to bounce back from setbacks easily. His feelings were not hurt as easily as someone with a narrower chin.

Face

Shape – Broad

He had a natural self-confidence and gave the appearance of having great strength and power.

Broad Face/Square Chin	He was a person that liked to do mental work in connection with some form of physical or mechanical activity. He was an active doer who loved to plan projects.

Facial Dominance

Large Middle Zone	He was someone who focused on status, luxury, and quality. He was very ambitious in completing his goals and dreams, but what he really wanted was to be envied by others for his successes.

Head Category

Low Forehead/ High Crown	He was unusually skeptical and demanded facts for the basis of his decisions. He was determined, dominating, persistent, and hard to influence. He was comfortable with power.

Lines

Two Short Vertical Between the Eyebrows	He was very hard on himself, a self-critic that set high standards and demanded more of himself and of those around him. He was always doing everything possible to make sure he was right and not caught off guard.
Indents At Each Corner Of The Mouth – Secrets	There were some secrets in his life that were very taboo—secrets he would never allow to come out into the open.

Harry Perdew, Ph.D.

Feature Checklist

Facial Coloring (page 25)

	☐ Light Colored	☐ Dark Colored	

Hair and Skin (page 27)

	☐ Fine Hair and Skin	☐ Coarse Hair and Skin	☐ Combination Hair and Skin	
Facial Hair	☐ Mustaches	☐ Beards	☐ Bangs	

Forehead (page 32)

	☐ Round and Full	☐ Slopes Back	☐ Flat	☐ Wide
	☐ Narrow	☐ High	☐ Low	☐ Brow Ridge

Eyebrows (page 37)

Shape	☐ Straight	☐ Curved	☐ Arched	
Distance	☐ Lowbrow	☐ Highbrow	☐ Middlebrow	
Distribution	☐ Starters	☐ Enders	☐ Eveners	☐ Unibrow
	☐ Access Hairs	☐ Chameleon	☐ Tangled	☐ Executive
	☐ Thick	☐ Thin		

Eyes (page 48)

Spacing	☐ Wide	☐ Narrow		
Size	☐ Large	☐ Small		
Emotion	☐ Stress	☐ Rage		
Angle	☐ Up	☐ Down	☐ Level	
Depth	☐ Bulging	☐ Recessed		
Color	☐ Blue	☐ Green	☐ Brown	☐ Hazel
	☐ Gray	☐ Black		
Eyelids – Upper	☐ Thick	☐ Thin	☐ None Visible	
Eyelids – Lower	☐ Straight	☐ Curved	☐ Very Curved	
Eyelashes	☐ Long	☐ Short		
Eye Padding	☐ Moderate	☐ Heavy		

Nose (page 61)				
Size	☐ Large	☐ Small	☐ Long	☐ Short
Shape	☐ Straight	☐ Concave	☐ Convex	
Ridge	☐ No Ridge	☐ High	☐ Wide	
Width	☐ Wide	☐ Narrow		
Tip	☐ Turns Up	☐ Turns Up Pointed	☐ Level	☐ Turns Down
	☐ Turns Down Pointed	☐ Large Ball	☐ Small Ball	☐ Pointed
	☐ Thin	☐ Notched		
Nostrils	☐ Large	☐ Small	☐ Long	☐ Flared
	☐ Round	☐ Rectangular	☐ Triangular	
Septum	☐ Long	☐ Short		
Philtrum	☐ Defined	☐ Flat		
Ears (page 77)				
Size	☐ Large	☐ Small		
Helixes	☐ Prominent Outer	☐ Prominent Inner	☐ Even	☐ No Definition
Placement	☐ Vertical	☐ Angled	☐ Stick Out	☐ Close to Head
Lobes	☐ Large	☐ Small	☐ Crease	
Shape	☐ Rounded	☐ Straight		
Height	☐ High	☐ Low		
Cheeks (page 86)				
	☐ High	☐ Full	☐ Narrow	☐ Wide
	☐ Sunken	☐ Healer		
Mouth (page 90)				
Size	☐ Large	☐ Small		
Angle	☐ Up Turned	☐ Straight	☐ Down Turned	
Lips	☐ Full	☐ Full Lower	☐ Full Upper	☐ Thin
Teeth	☐ Even	☐ Gap	☐ Big Front	☐ Crooked

Harry Perdew, Ph.D.

Jaw (page 98)				
	☐ Wide	☐ Narrow	☐ Jowls	

Chin (page 100)				
	☐ Large	☐ Small	☐ Sticks Out	☐ Receding
	☐ Broad	☐ Very Broad	☐ Long	☐ Round
	☐ Straight	☐ Pointed	☐ Very Pointed	

Face Shapes (page 106)				
Shape	☐ Broad	☐ Thin	☐ Diamond	☐ Trapezoidal
	☐ Flat			
Face Category	☐ Large Square Face–Physical	☐ Narrow Face– Thinker	☐ Round Face–Emotional	☐ Broad Face/Square Chin–Thinker/Physical
	☐ High Broad Forehead/Round Chin–Thinker/Emotional	☐ Square Face/Round Chin –Physical/Emotional		
Facial Dominance	☐ Large Upper Zone	☐ Small Upper Zone	☐ Large Middle Zone	☐ Small Middle Zone
	☐ Large Lower Zone	☐ Small Lower Zone		
Profiles	☐ Convex	☐ Moderately Convex	☐ Very Convex	☐ Concave
	☐ Very Concave	☐ Balanced	☐ Convex-Concave	☐ Concave-Convex

Head Category	☐ Low Forehead/ High Crown	☐ High Forehead/Low Crown	☐ Round	☐ Square

Lines and Marks (page 122)

Forehead	☐ Multiple Horizontal	☐ Single Horizontal	☐ Vertical or Diagonal	☐ Single Vertical
Between Eyebrows	☐ Two Short Vertical	☐ Three or More Vertical	☐ Triangle	☐ Several Fine Horizontal
	☐ Single Horizontal			
Other Lines	☐ Radiate from Eyes	☐ Diagonal on Cheeks	☐ Nose Wrinkles	☐ Nose to Mouth
	☐ Mouth to Chin	☐ Dimple Lines	☐ Vertical on Upper Lip	☐ Chin to Cheeks
	☐ Chin Arch	☐ Mouth Crescents	☐ Chin Bumps	
Dimples and Clefts	☐ Cheek Dimples	☐ Chin Dimple	☐ Chin Cleft	☐ Nose Cleft
	☐ Moles			
	☐ Birthmarks			
	☐ Blemishes			

For a printable Checklist email the author at info@harryperdew.com.

Simply type "Checklist" on the subject line.

Photo Credits

Page 7   Charlene Azcarate-Perdew, TPG

Page 16   The Marquardt Beauty Mask illustra-
                tions are copyright 2001 by Dr. Stephen
                Marquardt Beauty Analysis, Inc., and
                are used by permission.

Page 164   David Conover Sr., dconover.com
                Use by permission David Conover, Jr.

Research References

The Master Piece of Aristotle, Displaying the Secrets of Nature in the Generation of Man. Thirty-Fifth Edition. Printed and Sold by the Company of Booksellers, 1772.

Essays on physiognomy: for the promotion of the knowledge and the love of mankind. Written by John Casper Lavater, printed by C. Whittingham, 1804.

Chaucer and the Mediaeval Sciences. 2d ed., by Walter Clyde Curry. New York: Barnes & Noble, 1960.

The science of physiognomy, theoretical and practical: being a complete treatise based on Mary Olmstead Stanton's system of physiognomy adapted to present-day requirements, by John Spon. London: Herbert Jenkins, 1947.

About Faces: the Evolution of the Human Face, by Terry Landau. Random House, 1989.

When Heads were Headlines, Anthony A. Walsh, Ph.D. Department of Psychology, Salve Regina University, Newport, RI 02804 September 12, 1999 (1982).

Secrets of the Face, by Lailan Young. Boston: Little, Brown, 1984.

The Naked Face – The Essential Guide to Reading Faces, by Lailan Young. New York: St. Martin's Press, 1993.

Amazing Face Reading – An Illustrated Encyclopedia for Reading Faces, by Mac Fulfer, J.D. 1996.

The Power of Face Reading, by Rose Rosetree. Women's Intuition Worldwide, 2001.

Wrinkles Are God's Makeup – How you can find meaning in your evolving face, by Rose Rosetree. Women's Intuition Worldwide, 2003.

Face Reading, by Joel Lawson, 2003.

You Can Read a Face Like a Book, by Naomi R. Tickle. Daniels Publishing, 2003.

SUGGESTED READING

Amazing Face Reading – An Illustrated Encyclopedia for Reading Faces, by Mac Fulfer, J.D.

Probably the best reference for practical face reading. Very detailed and well written. A must read for the serious face reader.

The Power of Face Reading, by Rose Rosetree

An excellent, well-written book with a holistic view of face reading.

You Can Read a Face Like a Book – How Reading Faces Helps You Succeed in Business and Relationships, by Naomi R. Tickle

A very good book on face reading based on the Edward Jones school of physiognomy.

It's More Than Words Reading People From The Outside In

Face Reading Seminars, Workshops and Courses

For information about face reading seminars, workshops and courses, call 888-719-6099 or email info@harryperdew.com.

Seminars, workshops, and courses are available for conferences, businesses, associations, and any other interested groups.

Personal and individual courses are also available.

GIVE A COPY TO FAMILY, FRIENDS, AND COLLEAGUES!

This book can be ordered from quality book stores. Or, use this order form. You can also order securely online at www.HarryPerdew.com

Yes, I want _____ copies of *It's More Than Words – Reading People From the Outside In* at $19.95 each, plus shipping (within the USA) one or two books $4.00 additional books $2.00 each to same address (California residents please add $1.55 sales tax per book).

Postal Orders:
Enclosed is my check or money order for $_____, payable to The Perdew Group.

Remit to:
The *Perdew* Group
P.O. Box 1446
Chino Hills, CA 91709 USA

Telephone orders:
Call The *Perdew* Group: 888-719-6099. Have your credit card ready

For orders outside the USA, call: 888-719-6099
Send to: (Please Print)

Name _____

Address _____

City/State/Zip _____

Phone _____

Email _____

I request an autographed copy, signed for: _____

Thank you for your order.

Harry Perdew, Ph.D.

Speaker – Author – Change Navigator

Dr. Harry Perdew is a persuasive communicator who speaks and writes with clarity, passion, and sincerity. He is committed to helping individuals and organizations improve their performance from excellent to outstanding.

He comes from a background of entrepreneurship and education. He has owned several successful businesses, taught at the university level, and directed a Small Business Development Center, which gives him the ability to shape the theoretical into the practical.

He speaks, coaches and writes on "how-to" skills development that enhances people's abilities. He introduces new ideas, like physiognomy (face reading), that create an atmosphere of possibility so that people can change their perspective on the spot and begin to practice newly learned skills. He believes this is a way for individuals and organizations to meet the ever-increasing demands of a global marketplace and the rapid pace of change.

9 781425 940744